JUNK

OUTDOOR EDITION

Beautiful

JUNK Beautiful

OUTDOOR EDITION

SUE WHITNEY with Kimberly Melamed

Photography by **DOUGLAS E. SMITH**

The Taunton Press

The Taunton Press
Inspiration for hands-on living®

The Taunton Press, Inc., 63 South Main Street,
PO Box 5506,
Newtown, CT 06470-5506
e-mail: tp@taunton.com

Editor: Erica Sanders-Foege
Copy editor: Betty Christiansen
Indexer: Lynda Stannard
Layout: Carol Petro
Photographer: Douglas E. Smith

Library of Congress Cataloging-in-Publication Data
Whitney, Sue.
  Junk beautiful : outdoor edition / Sue Whitney with Kim Melamed ; photographer, Douglas E. Smith.
     p. cm.
  ISBN 978-1-60085-057-8
  1. Handicraft. 2. House furnishings. 3. Garden ornaments and furniture. 4. Found objects (Art) in interior decoration. I.
Melamed, Kim. II. Title.
  TT149.W45 2009
  745.5--dc22

                          2008042139

Printed in the United States of America
10 9 8 7 6 5 4 3 2 1

The following names/manufacturers appearing in *Junk Beautiful: Outdoor Edition* are trademarks: Airstream™, Bakelite®,
Brylcreem®, Chevrolet®, Dumpster®, Ford® F150®, Goldfish®, Gorilla® Glue, Gorilla® Super Glue, Gorilla® Tape, Jell-O®,
Kool-Aid®, Lucite®, Mod Podge®, Plexiglas®, Project Runway℠ , Scrabble®, Scrubbing Bubbles®, Wells Fargo®, X-Acto®

WORKING WOOD IS INHERENTLY DANGEROUS. Using hand or power tools improperly or ignoring safety
practices can lead to permanent injury or even death. Don't try to perform operations you learn about here (or
elsewhere) unless you're certain they are safe for you. If something about an operation doesn't feel right, don't do
it. Look for another way. We want you to enjoy the craft, so please keep safety foremost in your mind whenever
you're in the shop.

To my amazing daughter, Elizabeth. You rock. Love, Mom

Acknowledgments

It truly takes a village to produce a book. As luck would have it, my circle of junking cohorts continues to grow in numbers and force. For this I am eternally grateful. You may be wondering who the newbie junker is on the front cover. My first sentiment of gratitude goes to my right hand, Kimberly Melamed. Her bright smile has an attitude to match, making her a delight to work with. Thanks!

Following me down the yellow brick road once again was Doug Smith, my camera-wielding counterpart. This man has a brain, a heart, and a whole lot of courage (a big plus when you're working with me). Thanks so much, Tin Man, from your friend, Dorothy.

Many thanks, Minnesota friends, for your generous gifts of time, energy, and locations. The Lemmermans and Doug Knoll were on board once again. Thanks for hanging in there with us! Our family hosts included Kathy Rose of Nature's Nest, the Mangans, Bergersons, Steve Kelley of Kelley and Kelley Nursery, and the Melameds. To the California crew: Wowsers! We came in like a hurricane-force wind and, like pros, you knew just what to do. Many thanks to the Hendrys, the Fullers, the Lindamoots, Paul Karlen, Pattea Torrence, the Thompsons, the Deithums, Chamelleon Furniture and Design, Francine of Remember When Too, The Cottage, and Pacific Home and Garden.

Thank you to my dear friend, Georgia Terrell of Georgia Moon. Mirror, mirror, on the wall, who's the fairest junker of them all? Gogo, Jojo! To my Airstream buddies, Stephanie, John, and Ruby Hendry; here's to you for sharing your family, your home, your junk, and even the little something I forgot at the cover shoot. You guys are the best!

Rick and Rebecky, thanks so much for your hospitality and patio memories at the Sea Side Motel (relax@seasidemotel.com). You are true friends.

Thanks again to my two East Coast connections, editor Erica Sanders-Foege and agent Susan Ginsburg. Without their friendship, expertise, and encouragement, publication of this book would not have been possible.

To our four-legged friends, Dozer, Sir Henry, and the cover junkyard dog, Shadow. Thanks for the memories.

And last, but most important, all my love goes to my darling daughter, Elizabeth Whitney, and to Keavy Mangan, who kept a close watch over my little one while I was away shooting this book. You're good girls, too!

Hugs,
Sue

Contents

INTRODUCTION	**2**

PLEASE ENTER	**4**
Spring Fling	6
Summer at the Cottage	10
Fall in Love with Country	14
City Sidewalks	20

PATIO PERFECTION	**26**
Family Festivities	28
Tea for Two	36
The Living Is Easy	42

PORCHES WITH PANACHE	**48**
Porch for Three Seasons	50
A Country Porch	58

BACKYARD BLISS	**66**
Sugar 'n Spice	68
By the Pool	74
A Concrete Jungle	80

COOKING OUT	**86**
Contemporary Café	88
Cooking Poolside	94
Chuck Wagon Cookout	100

DINING AL FRESCO	**108**
At the Lake	110
Suburban Modern	118
Down on the Farm	126

SLEEPING UNDER THE STARS	**132**
Romantic Retreat	134
Family Camp	142
Midday Snooze	148

ROOMS TO BLOOM 156
Sweet Potting Shed 158
Seaside Garden 166
Meditation Garden 172

HOW TO
MAKE THE REST 180

RESOURCES 198

INDEX 200

Greetings, Junkers!

WELCOME BACK TO THE WONDERFUL WORLD OF *Junk Beautiful*. We're glad you're here. What's so remarkable about it? This is the place where dreams really do come true. Ask yourself this question: In what other world can you take absolutely nothing—like a barren piece of ground or an abandoned shack—and transform it into something not only useful but absolutely fabulous? The answer is—drum roll, please—only in the jolly old land of junk. This time around, we're moving our focus from behind closed doors to the great outdoors. So if you've been yearning to expand your horizons, come along for the recycling ride of a lifetime. On your marks, get set, go!

Our motto has been and always will be "reduce, reuse, and recycle." Not to mention "repurpose, refresh, and re-create." That's a lot of "r" words, we know, but these expressions have never been as fundamental as they are today. We feel strongly about using what we already have in our storage sheds, things found in sheds belonging to others (permission granted, of course), and stuff in the rough we've picked up at flea markets, swap meets, rummage sales, and other places where junk abounds. What to do with all of this rubbish? The possibilities are downright mind-boggling.

Let's focus on the subject matter at hand. The current nationwide trend seems to be running in the direction of downsizing the square footage of your home or, alternatively, staying in the same pot you were planted in and making it the best it can be. We say bravo to that! Scaling back at the homestead is admirable, but it may leave you feeling a little cramped for space. If this strikes a chord with you, we have some ideas to relieve your sense of confinement.

To get things started, please get off your chair (unless you read standing up), open your front door, and take a look at what surrounds your abode. Whoa! See what we mean? With a little imagination and some reclaimed treasures, all of what you see can easily be turned into extended living space for you and yours. Pretty exciting, huh?

In the pages that follow, you'll find bright ideas for outdoor living. From sleeping under the stars to dining al fresco and everything in between—including the kitchen sink—you'll find it here. Have fun and enjoy the fresh air.

Until next time . . .

See you on the junk pile!

Sue

IF COUNTRY IS YOUR STYLE, go ahead and choose playful, happy colors. Yellows and reds have a way of saying welcome home with a sassy, but friendly country twang.

Please Enter

What's the saying about making an entrance? First impressions are lasting ones, so make them good ones. We happen to agree with this age-old adage, so the matter of entryways was placed first and foremost in our focus on outdoor living spaces.

Do you live in the city, in a twin home in the 'burbs, or perchance on a rolling country estate? Guess what? It doesn't matter where you live; everyone has a front door. And with that door comes the dilemma of what to do with it. We have some thoughts on the subject as you'll see on the following pages, dressed for every season of the year.

The junk keys to success
are at your fingertips.

SPRING FLING

SPRING JUST MAY BE THE most difficult of all seasons to tackle. Flowers aren't quite in bloom, bushes are threadbare, and—let's face it—things are downright messy. What's a junker looking to decorate her doorstep to do?

We get up, get to the spring cleaning, tackle the planting, and without fail or further ado, we head out to the opening spring markets to get a whiff of fresh junk in the air. It doesn't matter where you live, spring just has a way of offering up the best junk selection of the year. It seems as though all of the vendors have been hoard-ing treasures throughout the winter, even in warm climates, just to get us hungry.

The anticipation leads up to a shopping extravaganza that's second to none. The goodies tend to be seasonal, so your entry-way will be in good stead after a day at the flea market or swap meet. If you are of a modern persuasion, look for interesting metal pieces to craft entryway ornamenta-tion and statuaries that will spice up your garden until the vegetation fills out. We think you might be suspicious at first, but in the end, you'll be pleasantly surprised by our selections for this entryway.

LEFT These chairs were "best buy" items. At 10 bucks for the pair, the original putrid brown color didn't dissuade us. A can of hammered-metal-look spray paint later, and— *ding, ding, ding*—we have a winner.

LEFT The clean lines of this entryway wanted junk to match. We went in search of and found objects that had no relation to the garden, but fit in as if they had sprouted right from the ground.

Sue could teach Michael Jackson a thing or two.

MAKE IT
PAGE 182

LEFT Garden art seems to be a popular attraction. Go to town with HVAC parts, threaded rods, and old outdoor faucet handles.

OUT OF THE CLOSET

Contemporary style doesn't necessarily mean sterile style. We think the term is wide open to your interpretation. Don't be afraid to have fun and express your playful personality in your outdoor living spaces. Go ahead, put it out there so everyone can bear witness to your style and the confidence with which you deliver it.

A combination of trash-can plant holders, musical backdrops, electric heaters, and a washboard is certainly one way to give your entryway self-assured individuality. Pair all of this happy junk goodness with bright flowers, a patterned rug, and polka-dot pillows on rolling chairs for a delightful look.

ABOVE **Washboards were ho-hum until we put one together with house numbers and planted it in the ground. Now** *that's* **something to get jazzed about.**

RIGHT **Light up the walkway with a candleholder that creates a delightful glow in what used to be the inner workings of an electric heater.**

WHAT'S THAT, YOU SAY?
Bike tire rims, cymbals, and
vents? This is not a figment of
your imagination, but it is one
of ours that came to fruition.

SUMMER AT THE COTTAGE

ABOVE An old-world thermometer with larger-than-life numbers allows even those of us older than 40 to make out the temperature without pulling out the cheaters.

LEFT Crafted from half of an old drawer, a frame, and some vintage letters and numbers, our planter is the center of all attention on this porch.

MAKE IT
PAGE 183

SUMMERTIME IS THE RIGHT time for everything pretty and pastel. This lovely cottage setting provided a heavenly backdrop to showcase this style. Our first focus was the doorway. A full pane of glass with divided sidelights gave us a clear view straight through the house to the beautiful blue waters that lie beyond. Now if that doesn't get the juices flowing, we don't know what will.

Many people still hold on to the notion that when summer comes, the best way to tackle the front entrance is to pack the place with flowers and loads of color. Although that works in certain situations, this cottage cutie cried for pure simplicity. We decided to take that route; minimal and masterful was the way to go. The minimal is summed up in three pieces: The watering can (everyone has to have one), a bench rest, and door décor was all that was needed. The masterfulness shows up in the door planter that appears to be floating on thin air.

Kimberly, happy as a gopher in soft dirt.

ABOVE **Check out the house numbers. Believe it or not, they were originally used to brand cows. We like them better used for this purpose—what about you?**

FAR LEFT Look at the little dude in the dirt. We have no idea what he is, but we love him just the same. We call him Welded Waldo. Pay close attention, and you may just find him hiding in other chapters.

LEFT Little birdies need food, too. Attract our feathered friends by placing food in a spool topped by a faucet handle.

BELOW The seating area takes its cue from the doorway and agrees that less is more. We call this "clean cottage."

This long and shallow porch had just enough space to tuck in a cozy sitting nook. Sometimes seating on a front entry is not all that conducive for lounging due to traffic noise and exposure to the public. In this case, the front yard was sheltered from the road by an enormous and spectacular tree, making this up-front conversation pit the place to be.

GIVE AND TAKE

In a small space, everything counts, so plan your pad carefully to make the most of what you have. The vintage glider on the facing page is big enough to fit three, and the fourth person at your party gets the wicker chair all to herself. Two chairs would have been nice, but they would also have disturbed the flow of traffic. Life is all about compromise. We did get to squeeze in a couple of tables. A side table and a wonderful old bench used as a coffee table tendered a landing pad for feet and a spot for your cold beverage of choice.

A beautiful lantern ran out of gas, making it a prime candidate to provide romantic candlelight on a perfect summer's eve.

FALL IN LOVE WITH COUNTRY

THIS COUNTRY PORCH is big, bold, and beautiful. If you have a big family, a wraparound entry will keep everyone happy.

RIGHT Help your little ones keep their stuff where they can find it. Looks like a budding cowpoke likes to keep his hat on a rake.

W E HAIL FROM Minnesota, so autumn is undoubtedly our favorite season. It's not too hot, it's not too cold, and at long last, the Minnesota state bird—the mosquito—is no longer buzzing and biting. Hip, hip, hooray! We can come out and play.

What can this Minnesota wraparound porch handle? Just about anything you can throw at it. Places to sit? No problem, gotcha covered. Storage? Your gull darn right. A hot dish on a hay bale? Ya betcha. The deck is so large it can even accommodate two kids on skateboards *and* the jump. We came, we saw, what else is there to say?

Large spaces are nice, but they can also be a bit daunting when it comes to styling. There are so many options it's easy to get confused. Start by planning just one day on the porch. How best will it fit your needs and the way you live? After determining that, it will be a snap to divide and conquer the space.

WORK IT

Now you're getting a good look-see at the size of the porch. Take a peek at the division of property that has occurred. Every place now has purpose, and everything has a proper home. At one door, we have a posh seating area comfortable enough to sit for a good long time while sipping a cup of tea and watching the kids raise a rumpus in the yard. The central locale on the porch is designated solely for the kid population.

Lunchtime and a quick game of Go Fish is what it's all about. The remaining entry is the portal of many purposes. It provides shelter to a seasonal hay bench, potted plants, and well-appointed junk sideliners. With room to spare, it also gives jackets, hats, and the woodpile a place to hang.

ABOVE Windmills of all sizes and colors are a junk staple in the Midwest. When the blades spin like crazy, you best head inside.

LEFT Baby Adirondacks are adorable, but if and when you get the opportunity to get your hands on one built for two, take it!

RIGHT Taking a large space and making it feel approachable is a key to good design. Ample-sized furniture items will help you reach your goal.

KNOW-HOW

The art of mix and match is one worth mastering. In a country space, junk in quantity is more than acceptable. Make sure you change up the junk to keep it interesting. Choose items with different textures and looks. A combination of metal, wicker, woods of different colors, and the bounties of nature will make your porch a pretty place.

HOW-TO
HAY BALE BENCH

DRESS UP YOUR ENTRYWAY with a seasonal project that can be stored in the garage during the off season and brought back to life year after year—with new natural materials, that is.

MATERIALS NEEDED

- 3 vintage rakes
- 2 sets of old andirons
- Bale of hay/straw
- Vintage or new fabric
- 3 long U-shaped bolts

TOOLS NEEDED

- Junker's Toolbox
  (see p. 181)

METHOD

1 Measure and cut wooden handles of rakes to desired height. Ⓐ

2 Hammer long U-bolts into the back of the hay/straw bale to hold up rakes. Ⓑ

3 Place hay/straw bale onto the andirons, spreading them out as necessary to balance the bale. Ⓒ

4 Slide the cut handles of the rakes into the U-bolts to stand rakes upright.

5 Add vintage or new fabric to the top for a cozy little bench.

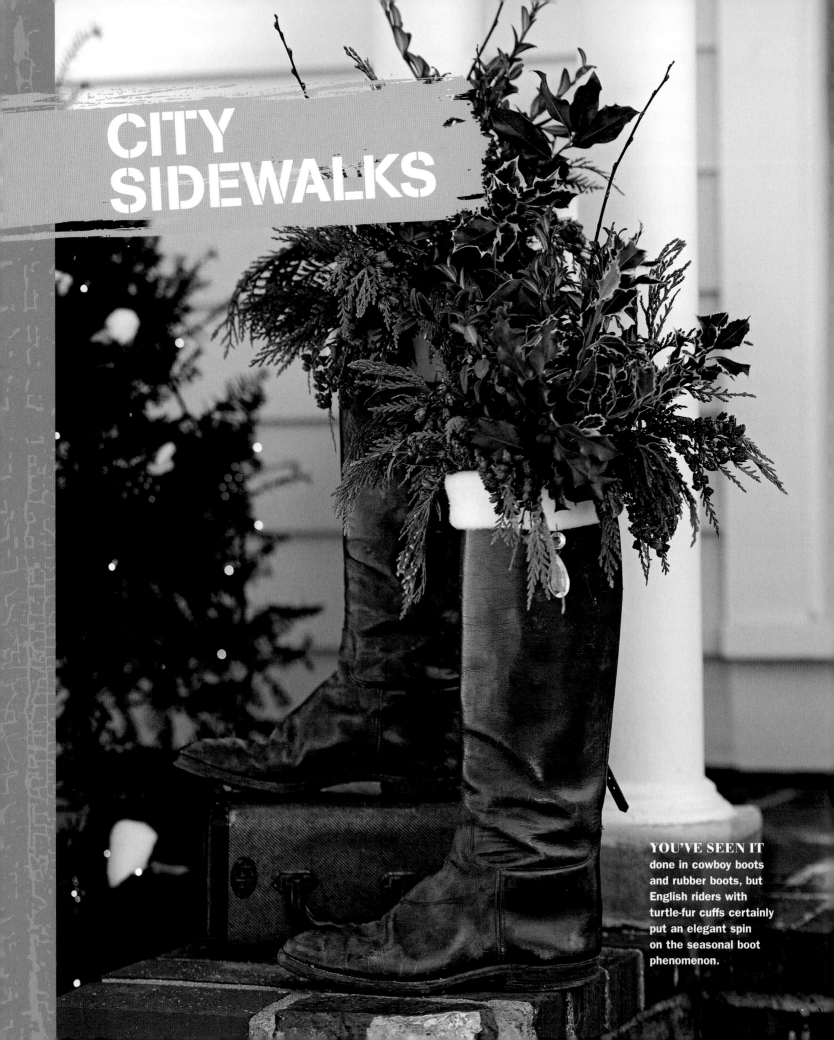

CITY SIDEWALKS

YOU'VE SEEN IT done in cowboy boots and rubber boots, but English riders with turtle-fur cuffs certainly put an elegant spin on the seasonal boot phenomenon.

IMAGINE STROLLING DOWN a city sidewalk on a gentle, snowy winter evening. If all was right in your world, what would you see? Do you envision glitz, glam, bling, blown-up snowpeople, and bright, flashy lights? Or do you find that mental image a bit disturbing?

Although festive décor has its place, we'd like to introduce an approach to a winter wonderland that's a little more subtle. Not so much Griswold (think National Lampoon's *Christmas Vacation),* but a little more in the direction of old-fashioned good taste. This plan of attack will save on precious energy and won't blind the carolers as they approach your front door.

This small city entryway is a good example of the art of merry moderation. In an effort not to overwhelm this covered entrance, we directed our focus on a few key areas. The items we chose were smaller in scale. For illustration purposes, the tree you see is actually a topper that might be used in a window box or to fill part of a planter on a larger portal. The other selected areas include the door and just one of the brick sidewalls. Temperance rules again!

LEFT Kiss me, you fool! Don't forget to put greenery that stipulates a smooch in your winter entryway. Hang it from a vintage scale for good measure.

BELOW We know it's hard, particularly around the holidays, but please restrain in a small place. *Edit* is a key word.

The right site of this entry offered room to move. The column created a natural stopgap in the traffic flow, so it was a good place to do our thing. A small tree put up in a bucket weighted with rocks was our main course. We love decorating with nature finds, so pinecones of many colors, holly, berries, and the like were obvious choices as ornamentation for the tree.

WINDOW SHOPPING

The bare windows flanking the door were easy to bedeck. We purchased inexpensive swags and added the finishing touches. Berries, greens, and some amazing thread holders were bundled together with subtle ribbon and tied to ornamental iron. We floated the iron pieces in the center of each window and created a little holiday magic of our own.

JUNK GEMS

1. Old corkscrews are cute and wonderful embellishments on a green arrangement housed in a boot.

2. Put a smile on the mail carrier's face. A big key and a vintage watch face are unexpected and out-of-the-box decorations.

3. We spotted the tip of this paint bucket buried deep in a mound of snow. Our junker's sixth sense told us its recovery was well worth the effort.

4. The beautiful wood on this thread holder is warm and inviting, just like the entryway.

5. A little bling'll do ya. The ever-popular crystal is right at home during the holidays. Here it takes up residency in a boot.

6. Who says everything has to look like holiday trappings? Unanticipated elements like graphic gear molds put some personality-plus in the festive mix.

LEFT **This wee little tree was just what the entryway ordered. It added a festive touch without overpowering the porch.**

ABOVE **Antique iron gate pieces clad with evergreen swags are suspended from rusty chains to dress up windows flanking the door.**

LEFT Again, you'll notice that simplicity reigns supreme. A grate and a dappling of other trimmings is all this wreath needs.

FACING PAGE RIGHT Oh, jolly golly, we celebrate the grate! Round decorative floor grates have a multitude of uses, but dressing the wreath is one of our favorites.

FACING PAGE FAR RIGHT Crystals are like Jell-O®. There's always room for more. Go ahead and make fun of us, but we're not laying off the crystals.

MAKE IT
PAGE 184

CUSTOM CALLS

A wreath of green hung upon the door during the season of festivities is customary, and who are we to argue with tradition? OK, we admit that, upon occasion, we do break the rules, but not in this case. Remember, we're caroling to the tune of old-world good taste, and a wreath rolls with that melody. However, we do highly recommend that the wreath remain a thing of natural beauty unspoiled by over embellishment.

A major statement like a decorative grate paired with barely there ribbon is a good way to deliver something special with a tasteful touch. What's the finisher? Delicate crystals wired to the grate put a little twinkle with no hint of bedazzle in your festive door hanging.

Intern Keavy heads out to the job oblivious to the 20-below windchill. Youth!

**ALL FOR ONE
AND ONE FOR ALL!**
This patio made for
musketeers of all ages
certainly measures up to
this famous saying.

Patio
Perfection

The dictionary would have you believe that a patio is a paved area adjoining the house, used for dining and recreation. No worries; Webster's is not right about everything. As much as we say "yes" to banquets and bustle, we say "p'shaw" to pavers and placement. A patio can be positioned anywhere on your personal plot that you see fit. We cooked up some pretty cool courtyards in less-than-likely outdoor locales. A family gathering atop a retaining wall, a place to toddle tea outside a barn, and a friends' night out overlooking a horse pasture redefine the word *patio*.

Are you from the directionally challenged side of the Mississippi River? If so, pillow coverings crafted from vintage map towels will never steer you in the wrong direction.

FAMILY FESTIVITIES

We think that marketplace umbrella stands are pretty darned ugly, so we improvised with a rain barrel weighted with sand.

WHILE SURVEYING these outdoor digs, we spotted a fallow foundation perfect for future family festivities. Would you like your family outdoor fun to begin? If you have tiered retaining walls with enough flat surface to house you and yours, then what's stopping you?

This two-tiered space, found right under our noses, offered precisely what the family practitioner ordered. There was enough space to allow Mom and Dad a place of their own to kick back and the little rabble-rousers a place to kick up their heels, a ball, or even a can. Now this is what we call a patio with a playful-plus personality.

MAKE IT
PAGE 185

LEFT This wine barrel top bears the number 98. We have no idea but this might be the year it was produced.

BELOW Brightly colored vintage glasses can hold flowers just as successfully as they can serve up cool beverages.

THE BRYLCREEM® FACTOR

Coming from large families, we've always believed there is nothing wrong with some separation between the 'rents and the rug rats. But why go too far when just a dab'll do ya? If parents and kids each have their own slice of space within the confines of the larger whole, it creates a family unit that's as wholesome as Grandma's apple pie.

Our take on a picture-perfect parental pad includes comfy chairs, a palapa umbrella held strong in none other than a reclaimed rain barrel, and an out-of-date child's toy that scoots the beverage bucket back and forth, making it wholly unnecessary to remove oneself from the comfort of one's chair. What's the best part? Mom and Dad, while enjoying some downtime, are still within close reach of the little ones.

TOP LEFT Implement an outmoded fire extinguisher as a candleholder and smother your fear of the flame.

TOP RIGHT Graphic components like the emblem on this fire extinguisher bring a piece of junk up a notch or two on the coolness meter.

RIGHT Fermenting in a barn for years made this pipe and gauge ripe and ready for a position in the ice bucket brigade.

In a world seemingly gone harsh, it's important to remember that when life hands you a broken rain barrel, make it an umbrella stand. A design scheme with plenty of whimsical elements is sure to put great big brownie smiles on the faces of those who dwell in these quirky quarters.

How did we assemble the eclectic dramatis personae of patio junk? A fast and furious on-location treasure hunt bestowed all of the goodies needed to make the patio this home's hot spot.

Re-purposing items found about your home will accomplish two chores at once. A new space for you and yours will be created in a jiffy for all to enjoy, and that much-needed space to park your car in the garage will become available.

AN INNER CHILD LIVES within all of us. No one can resist driving the wine up perched on the handle of a kiddy's red scooter.

RIGHT **See your Chevrolet® dealer today for side tables like these weather-resistant numbers made from discarded wheel wells.**

BELOW **Motel chairs are seemingly indestructible, making them ideal for the kid zone.**

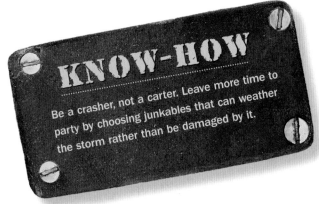

KNOW-HOW

Be a crasher, not a carter. Leave more time to party by choosing junkables that can weather the storm rather than be damaged by it.

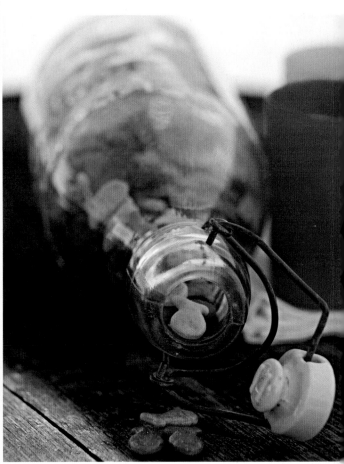

TIME OUT

Four well-mannered children lined up in a neat little row. All of whom are dressed in pretty little pinafores, short pants, and knee highs. That's what we call a filibuster on reality. Sorry, just had to take a moment to enjoy a personal fantasy. Now where were we? Oh yes, the peanut gallery's portion of the patio. It all began with the colorful motel chairs. It seems as though they have been around since the beginning of time, but they just never get old. After the chairs were in place, the rest followed along in capricious character.

One of the tenets for designing a place for kids to hang is to revert back to the day. We chose vintage pieces (we'd rather not call them antiques) that brought back good memories from simpler times. After all was said and done, a place was born where kids can just be kids.

Chim chiminey, chim chiminey, chim chim cher-ee! Kids are as lucky as lucky can be! Man oh man, what we wouldn't give to be kids again with digs like this. But who said that you have to be a child to enjoy such guilt-free giddiness? Absolutely no one. With that in mind, the fireplace area (aka cooker of white stuff on sticks) was designed for the whole family.

The chiminea can be easily stoked up, and all of the necessities for a good old-fashioned marshmallow roast are kept close at hand, cleverly wrapped up in vintage packaging. Remember, employing cast-offs creatively can add a new layer of cool to your outdoor festivities.

FAR LEFT **Chippy the chipmunk took a short hiatus from the playground to stand watch over the goodies at our family get-together.**

LEFT **Whoa there, kiddies; don't cross that dessert line before the main course. The school crossing guard is on the lookout for juvenile dinner delinquents.**

BOTTOM **For those nippy evenings, keep hats and coats nearby on a bottle tree made from reclaimed materials.**

A FAMILY GATHERING would be incomplete without a place to roast weenies or marshmallows. A chiminea is an easy fire-pit option.

TEA FOR TWO

ENCLOSED PATIOS
are for more than just
tending to plants. Carve
out some space and tend
to your own needs as well.

ARE YOU LONGING FOR a place to truly escape from everything and everyone, but don't have much time between soccer practice drop-off and dance class pickup? We know the routine all too well and do believe we have the answer. Step inside this sanctuary of solitude created just for busy moms. The well-worn structure and its abounding greenery set the stage for this feminine yet unruffled backyard retreat.

Women are creatures of many layers, and their havens should address all of them. That is exactly why we gave this on-the-go gal three options for the price of one: a place for morning tea, an afternoon reading nook, and an evening artist's asylum. Create one of your own, and you'll be glowing about the fact that you did!

ABOVE Pretty in pink, this sweet and dainty floral arrangement is the perfect side for your table and adds an unexpected but welcome touch.

MAD ABOUT ME

Ladies, there are those moments in life, brief as they are, when the world gets to revolve around you. Say, what? Yeppers, you heard us correctly. For example, take a look at our centerpiece, a tea table set for two made from a dolled-up electrical spool. Now, if that doesn't take you back to your college days, we don't know what will!

After the table was in place, we felt that a sense of division between the three separate areas was imperative. The beautiful screen doors (minus the screen in some places) filled the lady's dance card. Junk accessories were then carefully chosen to make the space not only beautiful, but functional as well. Cup of tea, ladies? One lump or two?

MAKE IT
PAGE 186

ABOVE The dainty teacups and frilly napkins were a fine choice for an all-grown-up tea party.

RIGHT This hand-carved sunset sign uncovered at a local antique haunt for a mere 15 buckaroos fits this space like Cinderella's glass slipper.

Speaking of tea, let's talk about serving it up in style. Our fresh-from-the-junk-pile rustic table sorely needed a touch of sophistication in order to hold its own in this elegant atmosphere. A silver tray from the attic gave us a good start. After attaching it to the top of the table with a lazy Susan mechanism, it was time to dress up the silver spinner. We added a treasured teapot, two silver baby cups for sugar, and a small bouquet of flowers to seal the deal.

LEFT Aunt Bessie's silver tray becomes a table turner for girls with a taste for tea. Pinkies out, ladies!

BELOW This is what we call crusty sophistication: a weathered stone wall, a cockeyed window, and PVC pipe planters.

*Angels of junk
before they've had their tea!*

JUNK GEMS

1. Washers, bolts, and twine are like icing on the cake of this salvaged electrical spool table.

2. A parade of little junk pretties takes its place atop a time-worn table.

3. This boot scraper is too small to handle modern shoes, but it is just right for holding photos of your little ones.

4. Try planting up a dish strainer from the 1940s. It sure beats doing the dishes.

5. A Christmas-tree-light reflector now brightens up the table as a napkin ring.

6. This vintage florist's sign adds plenty of old-world charm.

Some say that self-expression is good for the soul. We're big believers in this theory. Is there an artist lying deep in you just itching to get out? If so, carve out a nook or a cranny and set yourself free. This space is no larger than an itsy-bitsy, teeny-weeny, yellow polka-dot bikini, but we prettified the area with a nicely dated easel and a toolbox that was just too good for the work shed. The element of surprise comes in two industrial packages: a factory stool and a cool blue metal floor lamp.

TOP LEFT Forget the hammers and nails—this box is ideal for artist's supplies.

ABOVE Paintbrushes are a work of art in their own right. Use a glass frog to display them.

LEFT A painter's canvas comes alive easily in a space that turns an odd mix of junk into a perfectly palatable place to express yourself.

THE LIVING IS EASY

PATIO PERFECTION CAN can be achieved with the snap of your fingers. All you really need is some furniture à la junk and a few friends with whom to enjoy your unburied treasures.

LEFT Let's face it: The new hurricanes available today just aren't that nifty-noodle. These vintage glass pitchers, on the other hand, are.

I
T'S SUMMERTIME, and the living is easy. Thanks to George Gershwin and his brother Ira who provided us with the inspiration for this de-lovely patio. As with Gershwin and music, it was our challenge to create synthesis between different styles of junk while successfully blending the old with the new.

For instance, the cushions of our synthetic wicker set—a roadside freebie—were covered with swanky new fabric to save the set from the landfill. A decrepit old trunk of sensational pink and a table crafted from an unlikely combo of washboards and a printer's drawer rounded out the patio's furniture ensemble. What about the accessories? Many are local garage fare. Thanks for the help, George!

A TOAST TO JUNK

We weren't horsing around when it came to a backyard beverage station. As always, form and function is our motto. The hardworking three-tiered Hawaiian serving piece plays three roles. Funny how that happens, huh?

It holds the flowers for overall prettiness, presents the grapes for munching, and provides soft light during the evening hours. We chose some fabulous, midcentury glasses in a handy carrying tote and some to-die-for ashtrays as the garnishes for the station. This simple yet stunning watering hole is a fine example of how a mish-mash of cast-offs can properly commingle at a social occasion. Here's looking at you, junk!

LEFT We never thought we would find a place for the likes of this three-tiered serving dish, but when you make it multipurposed, it becomes a work of art.

RIGHT My stars, Georgia! When we found these ashtrays, we were tickled pink. The limes were quite pleased, as well.

FAR RIGHT Modern telephones don't require stands like these, but they do make excellent cocktail tables.

TOP This was a special find. Sprinkler heads are a dime a dozen, but if you see pink, buy it!

ABOVE These wonderful shelf rests from the Victorian era are a double threat as a candleholder and vase.

RIGHT This coffee break is brought to you by the handsome coffee service. Its credentials are circa swap meet 2008.

OLD WASHBOARDS AND PRINTER'S drawers are like the deer population in Minnesota: They're running rampant. We removed some from the wild to provide you with a humane alternative for control.

MATERIALS NEEDED

- Old printer's drawer
- 2 old washboards, standard size
- 1-in. by ½-in. scrap wood or new wood
- Sand
- 3 pieces premeasured and precut ¼-in. glass
- Skidmore's Woodfinish Cleaner
- 4 screws

TOOLS NEEDED

- Nail gun
- Junker's Toolbox (see p. 181)

METHOD

1 Cut bottom legs off both washboards to identical heights. (Ours are 18 in. tall.)

2 Measure and cut four 1-in. by ½-in. pieces of scrap wood or new wood, each 24½ in. long.

3 With nail gun or hammer and nails, attach two 24½-in. pieces of wood to top of washboards (one on each side) to create a support frame.

4 With nail gun or hammer and nails, attach the remaining wood pieces to the bottom of the washboard (one on each side) to create a bottom frame.

5 Set printer's drawer on top of washboard and top frame.

6 Screw printer's drawer to each of the four top corners of the frame. This should leave a 3-in. overhang on each end.

7 Clean wood with Skidmore's Woodfinish Cleaner, if desired.

8 Fill compartments of printer drawer with sand.

9 Place premeasured and precut glass over each of the three large sections.

COMFORT IS THE
name of the game when
it comes to front porches.
This seating area delivers
the cush for your tush!

Porches
with
Panache

The porch is a time-honored tradition among homeowners, and rightfully so. After all, throughout the generations, how many first kisses have been planted on the front stoop just before the warning light comes on to say Dad's on his way? We're happy to report that the romance with the porch is alive and well.

The ever-popular outdoor portal manifests itself in a wide variety of styles. There are far too many for us to show them all, so we had to pick and choose wisely. Which porches did we select for junk modification? We chose Cinderella and her ugly stepsister.

Gnomes are making a comeback and in a big way. We're delighted and hope that these happy little dudes are here to stay.

49

PORCH FOR THREE SEASONS

AFTER MUCH RESEARCH and undercover canvassing of neighborhood porches, we concluded that the backyard three-season variety seemed to be the most neglected of the species. We now lovingly refer to it as the basement of the outdoors. Like the lower level, the backyard gateway to the home also seems to be the recipient of leftovers. Can't find a space for it? No longer have a use for it? Let's put it on the porch. We're not exactly sure why this is so, but maybe the out-of-sight, out-of-mind theory comes into play.

If you fall prey to this commonplace trap, before too long you'll end up with a space that is overcrowded and put together with no rhyme or reason. We speak from personal experience. Knowing that every inch of space is important, we decided to tackle this catchall crisis. We brought order to this house by employing contemporary Adirondack furniture crafted from recyclable surplus skate-park building materials. Pretty nifty! With the major furniture pieces in place, the proper guidelines were established to finish off the rest of the room with high-style junk.

Thanks goodness for Kimberly. She can sew and smile at the same time.

FACING PAGE LEFT Straight from the liquor store to your home, this commercial bottle holder is spot-on for wine storage on the porch.

ABOVE The color story of black, brown, and off-white sent us in a more modern direction while decorating this three-season opener.

RIGHT Show off your family photos in style—suspended from a rack that formerly displayed the latest fashion trends in department stores.

The best way to approach a room that is under siege from the surplus army is to move the troops out, then assess which items will return to active duty and which will be honorably discharged. That's exactly what we did with this space. Don't worry, we didn't throw anything away—we simply reassigned. With a clear deck, we were prepared to move forward.

DETAIL DUTY

As you know, we're sticklers for the details. Those tiny particulars can make or break a room. Bearing in mind that our project porch wanted to bid farewell to rustic clutter and say hi to the clean lines of modern design, we went in search of suitable accessories. We unearthed our accomplices from a host of different junking hot spots, including the garage, to satisfy the call for contemporary. After gathering the goodies, it was time to give them new placement and purpose.

ABOVE These found bricks give new meaning to the phrase "if the walls could talk." Images of friends and family members are fire-baked onto the sides.

FACING PAGE We snared an old drum left behind by a child gone off to college and grabbed a spare from the garage to craft this updated version of the tire table.

KNOW-HOW

Several commercial retail store fixtures come into play on this porch. For this type of junk, check for used restaurant supply outlets in your area or read your local newspaper for news on business closings and liquidations. You'll find a whole new avenue to satisfy your appetite for unusual junk.

WET YOUR WHISTLE
at a beverage counter
made from a very cool old
restaurant wash-and-dry
station. Ice-cold drinks,
garnishes, and glasses are
all present.

OFF YOUR ROCKER

In order to entice homebodies off their front-porch rocking chairs and out to the back, we decided to throw a porch-warming party. A well-appointed beverage buddy is a surefire trick to attract attention. The entertaining portion of the whole is worth spending some extra time developing. You need to make sure that there's a home for all vitals and that what you choose to use can stand up to outdoor weather conditions.

Don't let the three walls of screen catch you napping. Rain, wind, and sleet have an uncanny way of breaking through those barriers. Selecting items that can hold their own against the storm is always a good idea.

HOW-TO
GALVANIZED VASE
COVERS

GUSSY UP YOUR CYLINDRICAL vases from the florist's shop with a one-two clip of your tin snips. Call it a wrap by slipping these bolt-bearing metal covers over your ordinary flower fare.

MATERIALS NEEDED

- A round glass vase of any height. Ours was 6 in. in diameter and 12 in. tall.
- Vintage galvanized corrugated tin, or new tin from the hardware store
- 2 #10 bolts
- 2 #10 wing nuts
- 2 washers to size

TOOLS NEEDED

- Junker's Toolbox (see p. 181)

METHOD

1 Using tin snips, carefully measure and cut tin to fit around width of each vase. Leave room for a 1-in. overlap. Ⓐ

2 Measure and drill four holes (two on each end) in cut tin to accommodate bolts. Make sure the holes align so the wrap fits tightly around the vase. Ⓑ

3 Wrap the tin into a circular shape, lining up holes, and, from the back, secure both openings with bolts, washers, and wing nuts. Ⓒ

4 Slide the tin wraps over the glass vases.

A COUNTRY PORCH

THE BUILT-IN BENCH was just raw wood when we found it. Add a few overstuffed pillows and *pow!* Instant country comfort!

MOVING RIGHT along, we're back to the Cinderella of porches. Most front porches have good bone structure along with the corresponding natural grace and beauty. If you want to enhance a front porch's innate charm, just give your local junk godmother a call and have her wave her magic wand. OK, maybe it's not that simple, but it's pretty close.

Take, for instance, what we call the Wells Fargo® front porch. Its enchanting character is what drew us to this location, but we knew it could be even better. The rustic structure and the countryside setting surrounding it stirred the emotions of our inner junkers and pushed us to design a front porch so cozy and comfy that it would be the envy of all others in the land. The oversize and well-stuffed furniture, lazy-days reading materials, family fun card games, and plenty of flickering candlelight all took part in making this pumpkin-to-silver-coach conversion a reality.

ABOVE **It wouldn't be a country porch without a garden bouquet. These perky yellow summertime blooms greet you with smiles on their faces.**

RIGHT **They don't make 'em like they used to. This old, broken-down donkey is the essence of old-style garden art.**

MAKE IT
PAGE 187

BFF

The porch, like a pooch, should be your best friend. Picture this: A small, winding broken-stone path leads you home to the waiting arms of a roofed-up outdoor retreat. We think the initial concept behind the front porch was to welcome you home after a long day and also to provide a place for you to slow down, unwind, and forget your worries for a spell.

To make sure that your threshold provides these rudimentary requirements, do it up in rustic refinement. Chubby twig furniture and fluffy Paul Bunyan–size down pillows teamed up with the sounds of nature will set you down the path to harmony at home. Once you reach your destination, all you will need is a pair of slippers and the newspaper. Where is that pup when you need him?

These little pigtails went to the flower market.

ABOVE **Lacy little farm flowers look lovely planted in a reclaimed bright-and-white enamelware teapot.**

ABOVE Even if you only have a moment to spare for a respite, turn to your porch. A few moments there will feel like a 15-minute power nap.

RIGHT There's something special about being greeted personally upon arriving home. Our little red-hatted fella does the job.

TWO STEEL CRATES STACKED, secured, and topped with glass make a pretty and practical coffee table for a country-fried porch.

INDIAN HERBS AND SPICES

Star Anise
Mint
Indian Bay Leaves
Cardamom
Fenugreek
Saffron
Cassia Bark
Nutmeg
Turmeric
Curry Leaves

JUNK GEMS

1. Tiny silver salt spoons tied with string enhance the natural beauty of an enamel teapot.

2. Make your container as sweet as the bouquet. Old bottles are darling when adorned with vintage baubles.

3. A camping coffeepot pulls a double shift as a hanging candleholder. Drill holes, hang with twine, and see how it twinkles like stars in the sky.

4. Come rain, sleet, snow, or hail, the mail must be delivered! But no junk mail in this pouch.

5. Old cheese boxes with their multitude of cubbies and drawers make for wonderful storage for the small stuff. Old Maid, anyone?

6. A vintage grocer's scale has all the bells and whistles a planter could want, including drainage holes. On a scale of 1 to 10, this planter gets the highest marks.

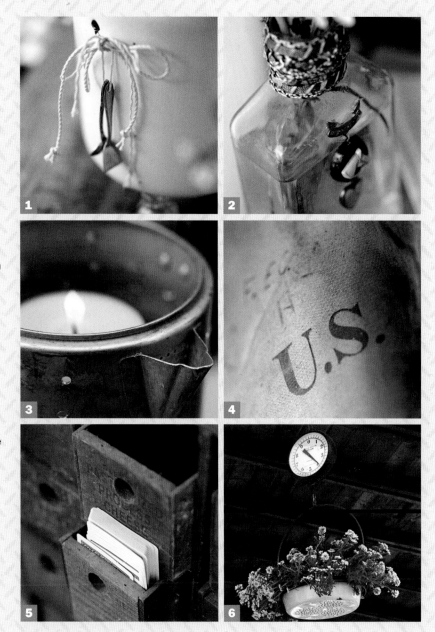

ROCK ON

While you're kicking back, you may want to have some things about you to enjoy and take in. To complete your porch ensemble, you can do one of two things: You can run right out and buy all of the newfangled outdoor accessories the hardware store near you has to offer, or you can go with junk. You know which direction we suggest.

Choosing the right trimmings should reflect life on the porch. Take your time, measure your decisions, and make selections that will grow better with age. Go to a few flea markets, take in an auction. Remember that you, your rocking chair, and your junk will be growing old together, so you'll want to make sure you get along.

RIGHT You'll be coming
and going through this door
countless times, so keep your
jacket and hat at hand on a
pitched-out fork.

BELOW A red metal base
(not sure what it's from,
but does it really matter?)
found lost and all alone in
the barn just happened to fit
a standard-size votive and
hurricane.

You can see that this front stoop is done up with all of the back-home-at-the-farm trimmings. The rustic barn wood walls with white trim, a ceiling with rugged beams, a sturdy homestead door, and lacy white curtains all add up to a happy salutation. Red is a traditional farmstead color, and we decided not to mess with an age-old country custom. We even stuck to familiar accent shades because it didn't feel right to change them.

BACK TO BASICS

The full-bodied framework of this structure calls for some rough-and-ready junk. The large all-season rocker and weathered red trunk are good examples of proper country porch attire. Adhering to farm fundamentals from color to décor will keep you steadfast to your country ways, and when the neighbors from down the road come calling, they'll feel right at home on your front stoop. That's a good thing!

LEFT We love the easy feeling this front entry evokes . . . as if you were a kid again and that family supper was on the table right inside the door.

BACKYARDS AREN'T JUST
for grass anymore. Gravel and
concrete pavers are a fantastic
substitute to the green stuff.
After all, don't you have better
things to do than mow the lawn?

Backyard Bliss

Front yards are for greeting, and backyards are for meeting. With that said, backyards come in all different sizes, shapes, and configurations. Some are enclosed city-size models, some are wide open to the great outdoors, and still others are gravel versus grass. Our mission (which we accepted) was to search out and rescue some of these different backyard varieties. After we found our open-air locals in need of some junkingly good décor, we had to put on the brakes—*screech*—before coming up with a plan for each.

As with indoor rooms, it's imperative to determine how your outdoor areas will be used. Do you like to entertain, or is napping more your game? For some ideas follow us "bliss" way to the backyard.

You won't need to go fishing for compliments when you spruce up your backyard buds with these very cool spools.

SUGAR 'N SPICE

OUR FIRST BACKYARD booty was short on space but packed with possibility. A shed with paver floors, pretty-in-pink stucco walls, and a slatted roof set the boards for a sweet and stylish nook that would put a grin on any cherub's face. Our target was to create a magical milieu where a child's imagination could run amok without misgiving. Ha! Who are we trying to kid?

This job provided us with the rare opportunity to take a step (OK, maybe more than one) back in time to re-create our own childhood fantasies. We put on the playground pigtails and got right down to the fun and games of making dreams come true. And some call this work.

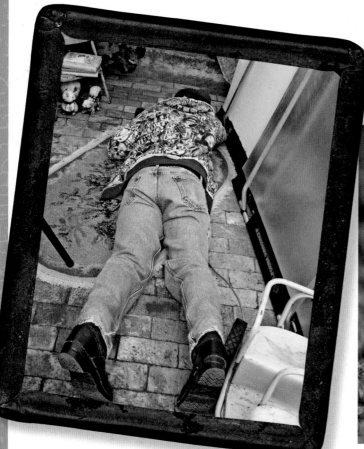

Dougie fell off his pink scooter and went boom!

BELOW This little fairy sprinkles her magical pixie dust upon all who visit this enchanting little girl's secret garden getaway.

ABOVE The combination of childlike
playthings and a more adult backdrop allows
this space room to grow with your child.

LEFT Tub time takes on a whole new meaning here. The Scrubbing Bubbles® have been replaced by soil-bound snapping dragons. Scary!

FACING PAGE The sittin's pretty when you cozy up on a sofa with puffy pillows and your best friend, Miss Pinky Poodle, and her good pal, Buddy the Bear.

MAKE IT
PAGE 188

LEFT Leftover wire from a broken clock? Feel free to finish a pillow with the weatherproof, commonplace cord.

When in a kid's space, use what a kid would use.

RISE TO THE TOP

Remember what we said before: Backyard areas need to work hard for their money. Knowing this, we were a wee bit worried that we'd be able to pull a rabbit out of the junker's hat in such a small space. No snafu you! We were aiming for and achieved three distinct rooms to romp, all wrapped up in one tidy little package.

Kids need room to grow and the promise of play to be fully engaged in their everyday lives. In order to fill the bill, we built a fairy-tale garden for tiny green thumbs, complete with a top-notch sprite and a sofa for playful surfing. Then it was time to finish what we started. How can you make nap time less of a struggle? Read on and see.

RIGHT This land of nod tenders an atmosphere playful enough for the very young, yet sophisticated enough for Mom's taste in décor.

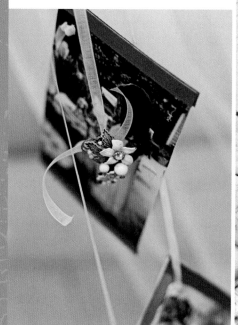

ABOVE Precious photos hang alongside family heirloom jewelry to evoke memories of yesterday as well as those from many moons ago.

RIGHT This wistful memory maker is crafted from a vintage lampshade frame, ribbon, and tulle. Make it special with your own treasured trinkets.

DON'T LOSE, JUST SNOOZE

There is no doubt that most little lassies have energy to spare, but sometimes power playtime can leave your pretty little pals pretty poopdee-dooped. No need to fear, the wonder junk bed is here!

Give your tyke a charming and comfortable place to lay down her weary head and gently fade into a world where dreams are made. Vintage blankies and linens offer a cozy curl-up-and-cuddle landing pad for sleepyheads. Books kept nearby on a stepladder and dangling doodles overhead are the only tools you'll need to send them off to sleep. Don't be surprised if you doze off for a moment yourself. Consider it a parental fringe benefit.

JUNK GEMS

1. An ashtray takes on the more wholesome task of keeping colored pencils within reach of the young resident artist.

2. The big bad wolf left something of Granny's behind to watch over the little ones.

3. This hand-crafted plaything made from a cork and a sprinkler head is tip-top on our toy list.

4. The hands on the face go 'round and 'round, 'round and 'round, all through the town!

5. Our mischievous little friend gets a little squirrelly for acorns in classic cartoon style.

6. Add some charming detail to your backyard play station by displaying vintage baubles and delicate feathers.

BY THE POOL

W'RE OPENING the gateway now to backyard number two. Any of you have pools or wish you did? If the answer is yes to either question, then we'll take you from the doggie paddle to the butterfly in no time with some swimmingly good junk ideas. It's a fact, Lifeguard Jack, that swimming pools and spas proffer potential for family fun from dawn 'til dusk.

Enjoying a brisk morning swim, basking in the sunshine, dining outdoors, or just kicking back by a roaring fire are all on the poolside menu. It doesn't matter what you prefer, just go right ahead, take the plunge, and pick your own paddle. We're only on deck to make sure that none of your favorite selections get the old "86" from the cart du jour.

FACING PAGE It's time to recline in the sunshine. Keep everything you need close by in a toolbox so you don't waste one drop of ray.

BELOW "Ice me up," said the vino to the Ice-a-Dor. Stay tuned for the chilling conclusion!

BELOW LEFT This old blanket was pulled out from under a vendor's wares, converted to pillows, and thrown into the lap of a poolside chair.

SPAS OFFER A GREAT
avenue for entertaining friends.
Make sure yours is well
provisioned for the occasion.

SPA-LENDID MOMENTS

Nothing feels finer than to be in Caroliner—oops, we meant to say, "than getting all warm and toasty after a long, hard day." As we see it, there's no better way to do it than by tossing on a bathing suit and slipping your weary bones into the bubbly goodness only an at-home spa can provide. To enhance your experience, make sure to be well prepared before you enter the babbling waters. Articles à la junk placed tubside will ensure a well-deserved moment of quiet relaxation. Close your peepers and think about the Big Dipper, candlelight, and a refreshing iced beverage. Sounds delightful, eh? Oh, before we forget, don't overlook the need for a towel after soaking. There's really no reason to shock the system; reality will set in soon enough.

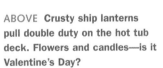

ABOVE Crusty ship lanterns pull double duty on the hot tub deck. Flowers and candles—is it Valentine's Day?

TOP RIGHT For the very best drink you've ever made, make sure the plastic pitcher says Kool-Aid®. Fifties moms approve!

RIGHT Freshly harvested from a local hatchery, these chicken-watering devices make cagey candleholders for your hot-tubbing delight.

HIT THE DECK RUNNING!

This poolside promenade of cast-off creations is anything but all wet. We've said it before and we'll say it again: Be at the ready for whatever may float your way. While designing this back-alley poolside retreat, we tried to look at things from a personal point of view.

Our subject, Professor Pool, was very traditional in her ways and expected nothing less than the proper junk curriculum to smarten up the surroundings. Good thing for us, we earned straight A's in advanced junking. Whew!

If you, too, are more of an old-school conservative, then we suggest selecting junkables showcasing more of a time-honored twist that will work well with wicker chairs and green-and-white-striped awning fabrics. Don't, however, be afraid to throw some unexpected items into the mix. The professor awards high marks for those who embrace creative license.

All this delegating makes a girl tired.

FACING PAGE This cart was plucked from the posy patch but is no garden-variety towel holder. It has space o' plenty to keep all at the pool dry.

BELOW Think of your pool as an outdoor family room. Make sure it has tools to perform multiple functions.

KNOW-HOW

One piece of junk can suit many different styles. Green army-issue tripods may not appear traditional at first blush, but it's amazing what a coat of paint will do!

MAKE IT
PAGE 189

A CONCRETE JUNGLE

TABLE ANY THOUGHTS of going hungry here. A combo of a new table adorned with roadside acquisitions is a feast for the eyes. This bright and lively color combo is sure to make you smile even on a cloudy day!

WHAT'S BEHIND door number three? We can't wait to show you! This backyard beauty is a junker's creative castle in the sky. We were presented with a blank canvas (including the lack of grass) and persuaded to let junk be our ultimate guide. Hmmm, as you can imagine, not much encouragement was needed. This is the type of project that will truly get a junker jazzed!

The combination of gravel, pavers, corrugated metal, rustic wood, and colors that went pop in the night was crying out loud for an urban industrial overhaul with a touch of elegance. Where does a junker find stuff o' plenty for such an undertaking? Head on out to a good old-fashioned swap meet for all of your shopping needs.

TOP The D.O.T. was more than happy to let this antiquated road marker go, giving the birds something to hum about.

ABOVE Automotive supplies are always a good choice for an industrial look. A car jack candleholder? You betcha.

LEFT Bring a grassless yard back to the land of lush using a potting table well equipped with container-gardening supplies.

ABOVE This inviting atmosphere is shaped by mixing a group of eclectic finds. Everyone is welcome at this backyard barbecue.

RIGHT Try ramping up your outdoor décor with a set of "built junk tough" car ramps to house your potted pretties.

BELOW Adorable vintage plates and Bakelite® cutlery planted in a table of green is certain to ring any junker's dinner bell.

An urban outdoor space can be just as verdant and vibrant as a suburban dwelling boasting grassy knolls, leafy trees, and luscious perennial gardens. Sound like a tall order? Mmm, not so much. Keep in mind it's all about making the most of what you have. A well-laid plan, a junk outing, and a trip to your local greenhouse will get you moving in the right direction.

CONTAIN YOURSELF—NOT!

The plan here was to maintain the "coolness" factor of the gravel and concrete yard, but warm it up just an itty bit by enlisting flora without the fauna. Instead of plants and trees laying stake in the earth, they take root here in containers, new and old. Once the container gardens are in place, feel free to move about the yard and add your own personal junking style.

LEFT **This may not be Manhattan's Tavern on the Green, but who cares? A planted railroad cart is equally stylish.**

MILK CRATES ARE OBSOLETE for their intended purpose, but can be put back to work with a couple of minor tweaks. Casters, hooks, and fabric pouches give this crate a green thumb!

MATERIALS NEEDED

- Vintage wooden milk crate
- Vintage or new fabric, ¼ yd. to ½ yd. (always leave room for operator error)
- 4 casters (1½ in.)
- 2 single coat hooks
- Skidmore's Woodfinish Cleaner

TOOLS NEEDED

- Junker's Toolbox (see p. 181)
- Needle and thread
- Sewing machine (optional)

METHOD

1 Clean milk crate with Skidmore's Woodfinish Cleaner.

2 Measure and attach both single coat hooks, on one long side, evenly spaced approximately 1 in. from top. Ⓐ

3 Attach all four casters, one to each corner of one of the smaller sides of the milk crate. This side will become the bottom, and the crate will sit on end. Ⓑ

4 Measure and cut three lengths of fabric to create pockets for the two bottom rungs. Allow enough fabric to finish edges. Ours are approximately 10 in. long and 4 in. wide, finished.

5 Double-fold, press, and stitch each edge of fabric to finish.

6 Loop finished fabric width wise around front rung and hand-stitch. Repeat process on back rung. Ⓒ

INDOORS OR OUTDOORS, the kitchen is the heart of the home. This outdoor cantina is as warm and inviting as its indoor counterpart.

Blue Plate
SPECIAL 35¢

Cooking Out

The fresh smell of outdoor cooking is in the sultry summer air. There's nothing quite like communing with nature, chatting with friends and family, and all the while waiting with unbridled anticipation for that first bite of mouth-watering flavor that only an open-air flame can unshackle. Mmm, mmm, great goodness!

There are many different recipes for backyard chefs. Full-blown kitchens with all the bells and whistles, easy poolside cuisine, and cowboy cookouts are just the tip of the iceberg lettuce. What you're about to see will get you hungry for a taste of the good life, so grab your buds and let's get cooking!

A retro pie server from the local soda fountain serves up napkins, in place of the traditional fruit pastry.

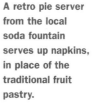

CONTEMPORARY CAFÉ

FULLY EQUIPPED OUTDOOR kitchens are all the rage, and we totally understand why. What's not to love about stepping out your back door and walking into a larger-than-life chef's dream come true? Believe it or not, many of these cooking quarters have more mod cons than their indoor sisters. What should you take into consideration while prepping for your outdoor cookery? Ask yourself, and be honest about what you would actually use if you had your druthers. For instance, if pizza's not your thing, then why waste the money on a pizza oven just because it looks cool?

Our point is to create a space suitable to the way you live. What are your options? They are truly endless. In addition to pizza ovens, the menu includes plenty of counter space, a refrigeration system, a cooktop and grill, a fireplace, dining quarters, a bar top, a beer tap, and, yes, even the kitchen sink. After your well-laid plans are in place and you're ready to take a stab at dressing your open-air cook station, consider junk as a complementary side dish. All of the newness that's surrounding you could benefit from old-style character that only junk can deliver.

RIGHT We love big, old schoolhouse paper cutters, but until now, we could never figure out how to incorporate them into everyday life. Thank goodness for pizza!

TOP RIGHT Vintage tins minus the rust are good candidates for outdoor flour and sugar containers. Most seal tightly, and they can withstand a few raindrops.

BOTTOM RIGHT After the dough rolling contest is over this nifty gadget can actually be used to cut paper. Go figure!

ABOVE We dug this out of the garden and believe it is a rusty old hose reel, but for our purposes, we opted for log rolling over hose reeling.

LEFT A big, open fireplace with all the junk trimmings is optional but preferable in outdoor kitchens. It provides creature comfort and keeps your guests warm.

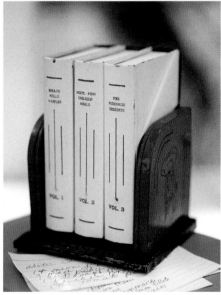

ABOVE Who would have thunk that cheese makers would put as much care into their molds as they did their cheese? We're glad they did.

RIGHT Direct from June Cleaver's kitchen to its contemporary counterpart, this neat and natty recipe card holder performs its original function.

TOP RIGHT This is a true junker's brainchild. A poker caddy without its chips holds small craft-store paint bottles filled with spices.

JUNK BAND

We were ecstatic to find such a wonderful and broad-reaching group of junk accessories that filled the holes in our kitchen wish list. We covered all our bases for these stations with an eclectic group of junk gypsies. None of them hogged the limelight, but rather banded together to form one fabulously functional performing group. Stuff from a one-room schoolhouse, a dark and danky poker table, a nifty fifties kitchen, and an obsolete cheese maker's storefront may not seem so good, but when we blended them together in our junker's mixing bowl, the result was one for the recipe record books.

The tip of the day is to try not to look at each ingredient individually, but to envision the whole. If you do this, your outdoor living spaces will rise to the top. Get it?

ABOVE **The counter space around the kitchen sink gave us ample room to store provisions in a convenient galley location.**

Sue waits patiently with unchecked expectation for the return of the pizza dough.

A PLACE TO WASH YOUR HANDS is mandatory in this kitchen, but a run-of-the-mill soap dish is not. A set of dominoes, glue, and a cement board remnant hold the suds.

MATERIALS NEEDED

- Vintage dominoes
- Cement board

TOOLS NEEDED

- Junker's Toolbox (see p. 181)
- Gorilla® Super Glue

METHOD

1 Measure and cut cement board with a wood saw. Ours is 5¼ in. by 3¼ in. Ⓐ

2 Glue nine dominoes, in a three-by-three pattern, white side up, onto the top of the cement board.

3 Glue three dominoes horizontally to the long edge. Do this for each side. Ⓑ

4 When the top and sides are good and dry, flip over the soap dish and glue one domino onto each corner for the feet.

COOKING POOLSIDE

OUR GOAL WAS TO LIVEN this place up without taking it over the edge. Unexpected items are the answer when you use them in moderation.

A FTER FROLICKING AT the pool all day long with family or friends, why would you ever want to get all dressed up and head to a restaurant for dinner? All the comforts of home can be found poolside, even the kitchen. It doesn't have to be fancy when fun and funky will do. Toss together an outdoor affair by using traditional things whisked together with some outstanding junk pieces. A one-of-a-

kind foodie frontier can be developed by using this method. Take a look at this very traditional setting for example. The white fence, brick pool surround, and stonework are all very lovely, but a little lonely. Thinking outside the fence brought us to the conclusion the junk a la funk was the way to go. So away we went. The bright pinks and greens in the towel and pillow selection gave way to pink flamingoes, tropical trays, and yes even some scaffolding!

ABOVE **This green enameled heater from France is a really spectacular piece and unbelievably beautiful as a table.**

TOP RIGHT **We love bottle collections. This is a fun way to serve your guests a refreshing summertime beverage!**

RIGHT **This flowered beauty was literally taken from its dirty trash duty and given new life as a pretty planter.**

RIGHT This well-used grill needed to become more functional. Using all of the available surfaces, hanging spots, and some junk, we crafted a well-equipped cooktop on wheels.

BOTTOM RIGHT A coal scoop is not too far out of place hanging under the grill to hold charcoal. Some things just never change.

KNOW-HOW

You know what they say. The best things in life are free. At this poolside party the old adage certainly applies. Some things can seem so unattractive to the untrained naked eye that they seem hopeless and end up curbside and lonely. Free, but still no takers. The next time you see an ugly duckling like scaffolding, pick it up, paint it, and rethink it.

SHORT-ORDER SUCCESS

A well-situated cook station was the short-order of the day and that's what we cooked up. The long narrow space presented a bit of a placement dilemma, but where there's a will there's a way. We decided that designing this outdoor cantina like a restaurant kitchen with line cooks was the way to go. Keeping the grill and the buffet in close proximity was a key ingredient. This made it easy for the diners to grab their kabobs, dish up their sides, and at the same time avoid any unanticipated encounters with the pool water. We dressed the grill with everything a backyard chef could want, and the service station had plenty of room for the rest of the goods.

LEFT Vintage linens are among our favorite things to buy. "Don't burn your paws" was an apropos addition for a grilling affair.

ABOVE New old stock (never been used) drill bits work wonderfully well for skewering veggies and cooking them up on the grill.

GOING GRIN

Swimming pool get-togethers are typically family or social events of a more casual and lighthearted nature. Cocktail dresses, heels, and stuffy attitudes are replaced by bathing suits, flip-flops, and playful pose. Much like an events personality your junk accessories need to fit the occasion. When it comes to fun junk, we're definitely game and ready to dive right in! If you see this type of décor in your future, follow one simple rule. When you hit the junking trail in search of poolside kitsch, make sure your smile is kept close and handy, in a most convenient place. You'll need to pull it out regularly while shopping. Look for items that put the whimsy in your world like circus glasses with pink elephants, sassy salt and pepper shakers, and comb holders from Bea's Beauty Parlor to hold your flatware. Throw it all together on a buffet made from junk and you'll have an affair fit for fun.

ABOVE **Retro glass lamp shades screwed to canopies are clever containers for food to be served up in the out-of-doors.**

RIGHT **These used diner dishes are awesome! The Downtown Club sounds like a pretty swanky place to hang out.**

BOTTOM RIGHT **Junk, on some occasions, is just meant to make you laugh. This pink flamingo is so bad it's good.**

MAKE IT
PAGE 190

ABOVE Shore up
your poolside cooking
essentials and keep
them ship-shape and
ready to go in one
convenient location.

An outmoded enamel cooker had to be good for something. Open the lid and the doors, and what you will find is a whole lot of storage space.

CHUCK WAGON COOKOUT

THE DINNER BELL is ringing, calling all to a fiery feast done up camp style. Holsters and saddles are accounted for.

Sue was last seen wearing a cowgirl getup driving a Ford® F150® headed toward Nashville.

ABOVE **Signage—you already know we love it. This one was too good to be true. It took us about two seconds to see it, buy it, and be off with it.**

NOW THIS IS SOMETHING to behold—an authentic, properly provisioned, green-and-red chuck wagon rolled on out and put to pasture in a grassy field overlooking cow country. This is a Cartwright-nice setting for a cowboy cookout to beat all cookouts. This type of campfire kitchen is for folks lookin' to take a giant step back in time and experience the way things used to be in the Wild West.

We were happier than pigs in mud to climb aboard this chuck wagon and go along for a riotous and unruly good time.

We reckon most of you don't have a chuck wagon parked in your garage, but that's OK. The ideas we're about to dish up can be played out in your backyard under a tent just as nicely. The fun is found in gathering up all of the cowpoke gear. I do declare we have never had so much fun as we did wranglin' up junk with western flair. After all was said and done and the cowboy cookery was in order, we sat back, smiled, and enjoyed the style that only cowboys and cowgirls bring to the plate.

RIGHT If you had to venture a guess between a deputy, a sheriff, and a marshal, which sauce packs the biggest punch?

FAR RIGHT Enamelware cups with labels are a collector's item, so be careful not to wash the labels off. Here they carry condiments on a spinning game wheel.

AS THE SUN GOES DOWN over the campsite, the fire gets blazing for warmth, ambience, and maybe a late-night snack warmed up over the open flames.

RIGHT When you're eating on the range, it's a help-yourself kind of gig. Get playful with your theme and don't let your guests be the only ones in costume.

YEE DITTY HAW

The food is fine and the weather divine at this chuck wagon special event held under the stars. Think just how much fun this would be for a themed family reunion, a party for friends, or just a gathering of immediate family members. Doing a cookout up right and in an "Everything's Bigger and Better in Texas" style will leave your guests and your family hankering for the next occasion to get gussied up and put the old feed bag on.

Who needs a vacation when you can dress up your backyard and travel to the land where saloons and dance halls still exist? With a little ingenuity and a holster full of junk, you will achieve success. Word's sure to travel fast about your ability to put on a backyard barbie, so be expecting stagecoaches full of western-clad weekenders to show up at your saddle post come Saturday night.

GRUB'S ON!

We had a great time putting some refinement to things that, back in the day, may have been a little rougher around the edges. Just because you're re-enacting a western ritual does not mean you have to live without modern-day conveniences and that you can't have a little fun setting the table. Surprise your guests with your cowgal creativity and go out on a limb when concocting your table couture.

We can assure you, after shopping for western stuff in the rough, we learned a thing or two. Folks who wear 10-gallon hats and big silver-buckled belts are not the retiring type. When it comes to having fun, it's time to get sassy! What's good for the goose is good for the gander, so go wild for western.

FACING PAGE **Can you believe that a salesperson actually carried this pint-sized saddle around on sales calls? Hold a wine bottle with it.**

BOTTOM LEFT **We think these holsters work westernly well as flatware caddies. Pick them up one at a time or in pairs at antique stores.**

BELOW **These iron pieces reminded us of horseshoes, so they worked well with our western motif. Cut paper stock, glue to the back rim, and put a name on them.**

MAKE IT
PAGE 191

LEFT A cowboy camp-style cookout would be incomplete without a great big "C" to remind you of where you are. We're always trying to help.

ABOVE The back of the wagon is traditionally where the cooking utensils and other fixings for grub are kept. We further provisioned it with a few junkables of our own.

EXTRA SPICY

How handy is this storage compartment at the back of the wagon? You flip down the door, and all of the extras you need for rich-in-flavor and highly seasoned cowboy victuals are right there at your rawhide-gloved fingertips. The storage unit also holds cast-iron camp cookware, flatware, coffee cups, and a whole lot more.

Again, if you find yourself without a wagon, you can create your own at-home version minus the wagon wheels. Go to a junk shop and find a rustic cabinet top or a big rough-and-tumble crate with a lid and dividers. Start collecting cast-off camp stuff and keep your collection in the container. Before long, you'll have a complete set. Next time the mood strikes for a western get-together, you'll be plumb ready.

JUNK GEMS

1. A galvanized bucket is a natural for an ice bucket—without holes, that is! Bring it to table height by setting it atop an upside-down camp stool.

2. This red horseshoe is a beaut! Don't flip it upside down, 'cause it will bring you bad luck, or so it's been said.

3. This highly unusual combination of an age-old skateboard and a stirrup makes for a perfect towel holder.

4. It's amazing what you can do with a horseshoe. Weld three together, give them some legs, and boil up a pot of water right on the coals.

5. This old horn is the real deal. Hang it alongside the provisions cart to hold matches just in case two sticks aren't working out for you.

6. The coals are good and ready for marshmallows. Warning! Do not douse hot coals with water in a cast-iron cooker. We learned the hard way that the cast iron will crack.

Lonely without Sue, Doug decides to make himself a pie.

LAYERS OF flickering candles in cast-off containers offer a touch of elegance to this twilight repast.

Dining al Fresco

Close your eyes, put your chin up, and throw caution to the wind. Ah, the open air—there's nothing like it!

It doesn't matter if you're dining lakeside with the stars, savoring a sushi soiree with your swanky friends, or enjoying grub with the Griswolds, dining al fresco is the hottest game in town. Keep in mind that anything you dish up inside can just as easily be served in an open-air space.

If creating an outdoor cast-off café is on your honey-do list, let's get started. Begin by taking a tour of your property, then locating and laying claim to that perfect spot. An area with defining walls or trees is nice, but a wide-open space can work just as well. After staking claim to your plot of land, it's off to the races to find junk suitable for your dining pleasure.

A napkin wrapped up with a blade of grass and a vintage floral pin is one sweet embellishment.

AT THE LAKE

TAKE A CLOSE LOOK at our candlelit dinner ensemble. Pretty dreamy, don't you think? As with any great design, we chose an inspirational element that unlocked the door to the endless road of possibilities. In this instance, the beautiful blue water was shouting, "Pick me, pick me!" So, to quiet the troubled water, that's what we did, and thus our color story was born.

The setting not only determined our palette, but it also set the wheels in motion for the overall quixotic demeanor of the room. The eclectic mix of refined and rustic furniture was the first to arrive at the dinner party. A diverse group always makes for good conversation. Next, the tabletop décor made its entrance and fit in with the furniture group as if they were lifelong friends.

A divine dining experience should not only be a feast for your taste buds, but also for your eyes. The idea is to sit back, relax, and take plenty of time to enjoy each other's company. The delectable goodies that adorn this table are designed to do just that.

LEFT For ambient dining light, look no further than your own cupboard for mismatched glassware candleholders.

THIS OUTDOOR DINING room offers up everything your indoor space does with one exception: the kitchen sink.

LEFT Bouncy chairs from the forties are well detailed and incredibly comfy.

THE DESIGN STAR of the tabletop is a runner crafted from a vintage barkcloth drapery panel.

TOP **Doorknobs attached to a threaded rod keep the table runner in its place.**

ABOVE **Itsy-bitsy juice glasses are perfect as personal tussie-mussies.**

ABOVE **Dishes from a used-restaurant-supply store help lend new meaning to the term "blue-plate special."**

Once your dining room has been defined, it's time to focus on a tabletop to impress the most discriminating of tastes. The barkcloth table runner was our guiding light and set the tone for the rest of the ooh-la-la moonlit night on the lake.

DELECTABLE AND DE-LOVELY

Have you ever looked at a piece of junk and thought to yourself, "Wow, that's romantic!" We know it sounds like an odd concept, but believe it or not, junk can put twinkly little stars in your eyes. If this is your goal, an amalgamation of little pretties is what you are after. And have we got pretties!

Big, comfy chairs and oversize benches provide comfortable seating while the charming presentation of table toppers puts smiles on the faces of your guests. This combination is not for the weak of heart, but for those daring enough to believe that anything goes. A driftwood table, a barkcloth runner, vintage juice glasses, and champagne flutes may sound like a jumbled mess, but lo and behold, a masterpiece is born.

REEL GOOD DESSERT

After dinner is done, it's time to reel in a summertime treat like freshly sliced watermelon. We decided that the service piece should be just as refreshing as the treat itself. We stumbled across this little sweetie at a flea market, picked it up, brought it home, and gave it a little TLC. A metal frame and a piece of glass was all it needed to become a one-of-a kind dessert cart.

ABOVE **Sweet restaurant dishes found at a used-restaurant-supply store paired with vintage napkins serve up dessert in style.**

RIGHT **A useless hose reel is practical, pretty, and minty-green fresh as a dessert cart.**

FAR RIGHT **The next-to-nature look of this dining room is reflected in beautiful buds floating before a backdrop of sky blue.**

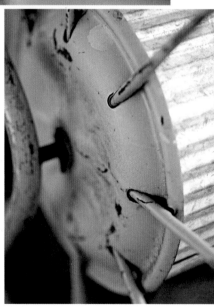

ABOVE **The carpet of green grass and the backyard's tapestry of gardens set the stage for this dining affair. Our hose reel cart was designed to work with the garden setting.**

Working with Sue?
Make sure you eat your spinach!

THE ETHEREAL QUALITY of this chandelier is what we were after. It offers ambient lighting for outdoor diners while not blocking the view of the beautiful lake in the distance. Elegant dining tables expect the same etiquette from their chandeliers. A collapsible wire laundry basket adorned with crystals and candles passes cotillion with flying colors.

MATERIALS NEEDED

- Vintage laundry basket
- ¼-in. manila rope (we used 50 ft.)
- Meal tray (ours is 14 in. round)
- Electrical cord
- Vintage crystals

TOOLS NEEDED

- Junker's Toolbox (see p. 181)

METHOD

1 Remove plastic casters with hammer. Ⓐ

2 Push legs of basket together.

3 Cut rope to desired length, thread through bottom of legs, and knot.

4 Measure and drill four holes evenly spaced around edge of metal tray. Ⓑ

5 Cut four strips of electrical cord to appropriate length (ours is 12 in.) so the cord is long enough to suspend the tray in the basket (as shown).

6 Thread cord through each hole and knot on the underside of the tray. Ⓒ

7 Tie each cord to top of laundry basket.

8 Attach crystals to bottom of laundry basket.

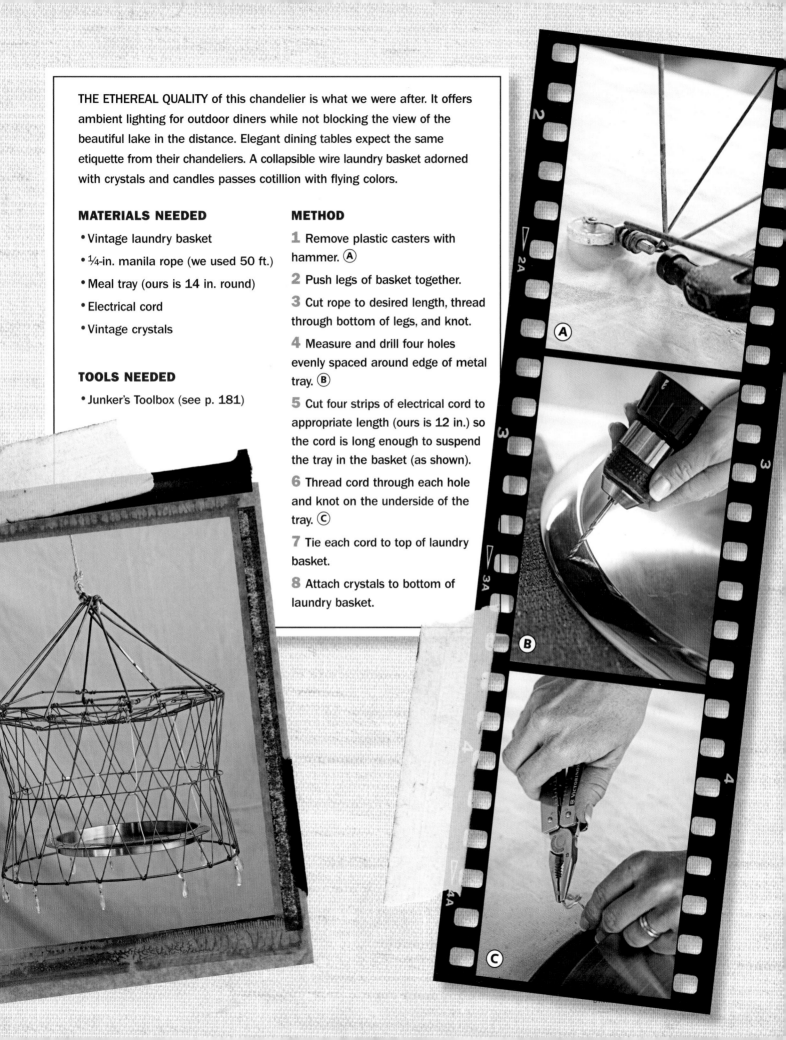

SUBURBAN MODERN

LET'S FACE FACTS:
Paper plates aren't all that
cool. Bamboo dinnerware,
on the other hand, is all
that and more.

THE TABLETOP IS THE centerpiece of every outdoor dining room. Much like a painter with a blank canvas, the sky is the limit when it comes to your creativity, so roll up your sleeves, put on your thinking cap, and go to town. Our mental vision here was to cook up a more contemporary concoction while also creating a sense of homeyness. Just another approach that comes with the junking territory.

We call this the "meatloaf meets sushi" design strategy. To achieve this look, begin by choosing fresh, crisp colors and blend them with the warmth of well-worn wood. An eclectic mix of tabletop accessories is also a must. This table setting is a fine example of something old and something new, making for a blue-ribbon recipe. Inexpensive plates, earth-friendly bamboo tableware, and a truly unexpected mixed bag of junk join forces to lend the fancy to the feast.

TOP These Lucite® drawer pulls have a dual role at the dinner party: holding seating assignments and chopsticks.

ABOVE This one will give you the giggles. A fish-filleting board and a roller skate team up to serve sushi.

One more turn, Uncle Jed, and I guarantee we'll hit the bubblin' crude!

LEFT **Crusty brown-bottle bud vases are a dime a dozen, but here they dress up nicely with wooden-float candleholders.**

BELOW **Horse muzzles and doorknobs make planters you can't say** *neigh* **to.**

TOO COOL FOR SCHOOL

Just because you've set the table doesn't mean you get to ring the dinner bell quite yet. Like schoolchildren, an open-air eatery needs some boundaries, after all! Frame up your space with schoolhouse doors (through which the dreaded principal Peterson used to peer). Make sure the doors are well grounded to avoid any mishaps caused by windy weather.

Once the perimeter has been secured, bring in a squadron of junk along with a few bits and pieces from nature's harvest to get your classy party started. A weathered yet modern pine table lays the foundation for the rest of our design curriculum. The mix of chairs—from wood to retro pleather—that surround the table and a gas station moving cart provide the extracurriculars. After careful consideration, we gave this room an A+.

THE PLEASING combination of warm woods, industrial metal salvage, and textiles shapes this contemporary yet comfortable atmosphere.

METAL RODS are attached to the top of the center doors, allowing us to hang junk planters above the table.

MAKE IT
PAGE 192

KNOW-HOW

If you see something of interest to you setting next to a Dumpster®, don't hesitate to ask for it! Our industrial cart was found at a gas station awaiting certain demise. An inquiry, a phone call, and within five minutes, the cart was safe in our trailer bound for better things.

TOP **Button boards are as pretty as they are plentiful, especially for our new sake tray.**

ABOVE **Believe it or not, this vintage clothespin bag, used here as a wine bucket, was our muse for this dining room.**

TOP RIGHT **The size of this cart provided oodles of room for all of our dining-out necessities.**

Take a little look-see through some pretty darn nifty-noodle chicken wire windows to what lies within. Food was meant to be enjoyed at a leisurely pace, and this room delivers some savory dishes worth lingering over. The dark, rich wood of the doors provide the ideal complement to the industrial metal gas station cart. Yes indeed, every yin must have its yang.

As you know by now, junkers find the good stuff in the most unlikely of places. While heading out to build this dining room, we needed to stop and refuel the junk mobile. As we pulled in, right there before our very eyes was the missing link. *Ding, ding, ding,* the junk bells were ringing. This phenomenon is what is commonly referred to as rock star junking.

ABOVE **Nature gave us the table and we supplied the rest. Two vinyl chairs, a candle, and a cool brew. What more could you ask for?**

Clearly, Sue's got a lot on her mind today.

STUMPED?

Before dinner, after dinner, or maybe even between courses, it's nice to have a place for a sit-down conversation. This two-person chat room offers a place to do just that and also creates a division from the rest of the backyard where the doors leave off. To get this look, try some big tree stumps on for size. With a little leveling, you'll find they make excellent side tables for your outdoor eatery. Next, you'll want to enhance nature. Wherever can you find these nifty fifties chairs? Look first in your own storage shed or one belonging to a relative. If you can't find them there, a garage sale is sure to produce some of these pleather beauties. Finally, all you need to do is top the table. A cold brew by candlelight is a winning combination.

ABOVE LEFT Individual salt and pepper shakers crafted from baby brown bottles are the spice of life.

ABOVE RIGHT These schoolhouse doors have great style all locked up.

FAR LEFT Watch the reaction this napkin ring garners from your guests.

LEFT Roll up the sushi condiments on a discarded wooden-wheeled roller skate.

DOWN ON THE FARM

THIS TABLE IS SET with all of the basics you would expect to find on the farm, but the presentation is anything but run of the mill.

FARM LIVING IS THE LIFE

FARM LIVING IS THE LIFE for us, doo, doo, doo . . . do, do! Nothing says "farm" like an oversize table all dressed with countrified junk and made ready for some real home-style eats and treats. When you're out in the country, everything seems larger than life, so the scale of the furniture in this dining room needed to address this issue. A ginormous recycled board rests atop an ancient industrial farm cart with rusty iron wheels. The big-and-tall-man-size rustic wooden chairs were plucked from the barn and put back into action.

Our next chore was to cover the tabletop that was large enough to seat all of the kissing cousins. We couldn't locate one tablecloth large enough, so we chose three smaller square vintage models that would do just as well, if not better. After that, we rounded up some whimsical but practical junk side dishes sure to put smiles on the faces of all.

ABOVE **A pillow covered with scrap vintage fabric is wrapped up with an old linen hand towel for added interest.**

BELOW **Colorful country kitchen bowls flipped upside down and paired with restaurant dishes make sweet candleholders.**

SERVE YOUR HOAGIES
up family-style on a croquet
set holder easily repurposed
as a sandwich board.

ABOVE **Slow down, you move too fast. Ya got to make the meal last, kids!**

TOP RIGHT **This little red wagon is a perfect dining table for your pint-size peeps.**

RIGHT **Enamelware and metal cups are cute and country-crisp accessories for a kids' table.**

It was sandwich time for the farm family's midday picnic, so a familiar family game piece like our croquet set holder seemed like the best piece of junk to dish up the grub. After we knew how the food would be handled, it was time to concentrate on where to eat it. That's when it dawned on us. Every extended family gathering tradition dictates a kids' table.

We took this ritual one step further and created an entire child's room. A wagon table, kiddie Adirondacks, and a galvanized bucket with apples for bobbing made this space a child's dream come true. We don't know about you, but we think you're never too old for the kids' table.

ABOVE **Red's the color of the day, so this Rock Spring crate was the perfect pick for a coffee tote.**

ABOVE **Come and get it! Make after-mealtime treats even more attractive by serving them up on a one-of-a-kind country dessert buffet.**

No, you're not on Easter Island. This is just really cool junk.

JUNK GEMS

1. Enamel bowls with flowers don't seem to be flea shoppers' favorites, but in our book, they're awesome and the price is right.

2. This tiny tot hammer toy brings back childhood memories while serving up an adult beverage.

3. Caramel apples are every kid's favorite. Try dishing them up with a baby fork handle.

4. This croquet set carrier has room for the sandwich, condiments, and vintage S&P shakers to boot.

5. Aluminum baking pans, red and white napkins, country store price tags, and blue feed scoops make for farmilicious dining.

6. The bobbing's never been better than it is with this French farm-beautiful bucket.

We suggest you follow Mom's advice and save room for dessert, particularly when it's presented in such an inviting and family-friendly way. There's never a shortage of straw on the farm, so we decided to borrow a few bales and make a sideboard with a natural touch. The straw needed some anchor pieces, so it was high time to hit the junk pile. We uncovered some very remarkable cast-offs that helped solve this picnic puzzle. The straw bales were mounted on an old sturdy packing crate and then sandwiched between two beautiful red cupolas.

The end result was a buffet befitting some family favorites, like blueberry pie and caramel apples, and some coffee for the adults and sodas for the little ones to wash it all down. Again, the junk pile was good to us and bestowed upon us some ab fab stuff, like a vintage crate, an old cooler, and a cool red coffee pot.

MOVING TO AND FRO
on a swinging bed built for
two—does it get any more
romantic than that? OK, we'll
throw in a starlit sky and a
gentle breeze for good measure.

Sleeping under the Stars

Research tells us that we spend a third of our life sleeping. Slumber is undeniably irresistible, and we inevitably surrender to its temptation. Knowing this, we put on our thinking nightcaps (the ones that go on the head, not in a glass) and came up with some pretty snazzy junk-style shelters for snoozing. If you're longing for a private getaway with your honey, a full-blown family slumber site, or even just a place to escape from your weekly lawn duties, you've come to the right place. Follow us into the land of midday naps and nocturnal nod.

Fore! Here's a heads-up for great candleholders straight from the driving range. Just add a hurricane globe.

ROMANTIC RETREAT

PEEK-A-BOO WHO?
The primary color story
found inside this door
is happy, yet makes you
want to nestle right in
and never leave.

H AVE YOU EVER thought about creating a B&B in your own backyard? We highly recommend it. Just close your eyes and think about it for a moment. How wonderful would it be to slip out the back door and retreat to a place where beds swing, candles burn, and bathtubs bubble? There's no need to hire a babysitter (you're only a few steps away), no driving nightmares, and best of all, no hefty hotel bill. Well, well, well. You're with us on this one, aren't you?

Our country quarters for couples all began with a simple and rustic screened-in gazebo. As with traditional bedrooms, our first chore was to come up with a bed for this nest. A simple box built with heavyweight plywood and suspended from a chain was an instinctive choice. After that, the rest was a nighttime breeze. A blend of vintage and store-bought linens fulfilled the fluffy goodness requirement for restful REM. To complement the couples cradle, we rescued some stuff in the rough without leaving the grounds. Tables, chairs, benches, and a host of other junkables were either repositioned or brought out of storage to create this inviting atmosphere.

Photographer's assistants have it made in the shade!

TOP **Extra, extra, read all about it! Plant a weathered bench outside your door for accepting delivery of current events publications.**

BOTTOM **Just for fun, accent your country duds with a more modern element, like this graphic vintage feed sack pillowcase.**

ABOVE Sneak away and enjoy a juicy romance novel burrowed in a pillow-packed Adirondack chair. How decadent! But you deserve it.

RIGHT Keep an old-fashioned flashlight close at hand for those late-night romps to the loo. Gopher holes can be brutal.

FAR RIGHT Apparently our good ol' friend Howard Spring forgot his luggage. We put it to good use for linen storage. Thanks a heap, Howie!

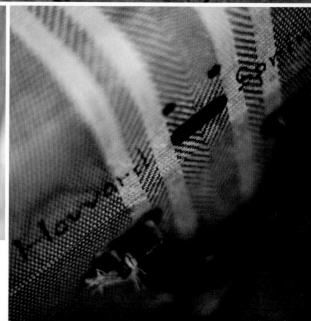

Before catching your well-merited 40 winks, you may just want to sit a spell and ponder, read, or just—dare we say—do nothing. For this leisurely activity, you will need a proper conversation pit. Keep in mind that, unlike us, some things just never get old. Tried-and-true blue country fare should include the customary set of Adirondack chairs. In this case, the crustier the chair, the better it is.

PUT YOUR CARDS ON THE TABLE

You can't sit comfortably unless you have a place to house your hideaway provisions. This box-top table is an excellent choice. The top is roomy enough to handle fresh-cut flowers in a lamp vase, a candleholder, a vintage timepiece, and your reading materials.

RIGHT **A rugged blue vintage box set atop brick legs provides much-needed storage.**

HOW-TO

TICKING
HEADBOARD

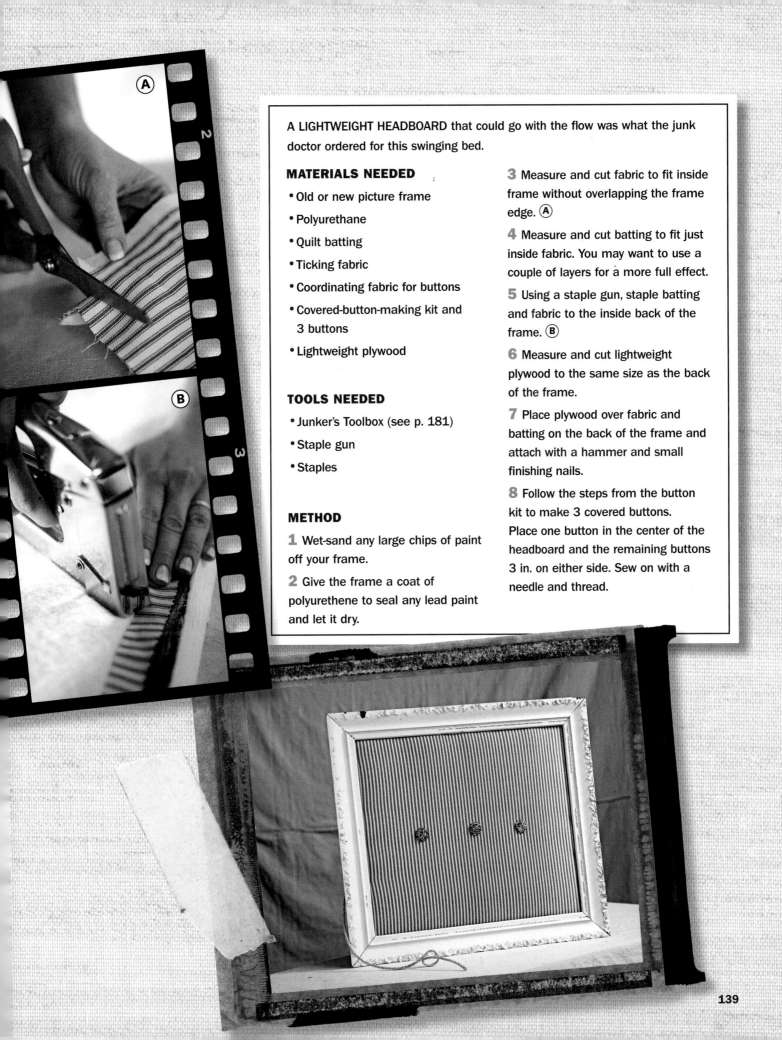

A LIGHTWEIGHT HEADBOARD that could go with the flow was what the junk doctor ordered for this swinging bed.

MATERIALS NEEDED

- Old or new picture frame
- Polyurethane
- Quilt batting
- Ticking fabric
- Coordinating fabric for buttons
- Covered-button-making kit and 3 buttons
- Lightweight plywood

TOOLS NEEDED

- Junker's Toolbox (see p. 181)
- Staple gun
- Staples

METHOD

1 Wet-sand any large chips of paint off your frame.

2 Give the frame a coat of polyurethene to seal any lead paint and let it dry.

3 Measure and cut fabric to fit inside frame without overlapping the frame edge. (A)

4 Measure and cut batting to fit just inside fabric. You may want to use a couple of layers for a more full effect.

5 Using a staple gun, staple batting and fabric to the inside back of the frame. (B)

6 Measure and cut lightweight plywood to the same size as the back of the frame.

7 Place plywood over fabric and batting on the back of the frame and attach with a hammer and small finishing nails.

8 Follow the steps from the button kit to make 3 covered buttons. Place one button in the center of the headboard and the remaining buttons 3 in. on either side. Sew on with a needle and thread.

YA GOTTA LOVE THIS: twilight tubs for two. What's even better is that they come complete with hot water.

Just down the road apiece from the main abode (about 50 ft.) is what we call the bonus bath house. No need to fear for lack of privacy, as the entire backyard compound is enclosed by a tall hedge. So throw on a robe and some slips and head on down to the bath, where the water runs warm. How's that, you say? The hoses are hooked up to a water heater. Isn't life grand?

BATHTIME BUDDIES

In order to ensure a suitable soak, dress up your tubs for two with everything you could ever need and then some. A hanging birdcage for toiletries, old pitchers for holding the scrubbies, and an enamel wall shelf that works just as well as a catchall on the floor are among our cast-off choices. With these in place, all you need to do is lie back and relax.

BELOW Thank goodness for naked lamp shades. If it weren't for them, we'd have no place to store our towels.

LEFT Let your thoughts percolate while enjoying lit candles held by the interior working parts of an old-fashioned drip coffeepot.

BOTTOM LEFT This most excellent old-world bath heater was a must for our backyard bathroom. No workie, no biggie; put a plant in it.

FAMILY CAMP

A DIP IN THE CREEK, fly-fishing the stream, or lounging trailerside: Whatever suits your fancy, we've got ya covered.

Land Yacht

ROUND UP THE RELATIONS, because we're about to show you what family fun in the summer sun is all about. Why send the kids off to summer camp when you can establish the same roughin' it atmosphere complete with the best qualified and most highly respected camp counselor this side of the Mississippi—you? And as a bonus, we will share the fine art of getting closer to nature without getting farther from the nearest cold beverage, hot shower, and flush toilet. After all, there are some things that remain sacred.

Our backdrop is none other than an Airstream™ trailer, but if you don't have one of these sleek silver bullets, there are plenty of alternatives. All you really need is an open outdoor space, some cool junk, a vivid imagination, and the willingness to be young at heart.

ABOVE **A kindergarten abacus holds towels for use after a refreshing swim. Now that's what we call elementary.**

Sue wins the challenges and advances to the next round of Project Runway℠ with this burlap beauty.

JUNK GEMS

1. Cagney meets Lacey. This retro lone buck sleeping bag paired with flouncy vintage linens keeps the rope bed under cover.

2. Madge and Merrill strike again. This infamous dapper and dynamic duo is on the "A" list for every sha-wanky shindig.

3. Staying up past bedtime is a rite of passage. Aid and abed your little rebels by shedding some light on the subject.

4. If you're fishing for compliments on your good-looking family, frame them up in a cod pole and put 'em on the dinner table.

5. Shake things up at your camp dinner table with some off-the-wall street S&Ps.

6. Keep essential Airstream reading materials right under the bed in an enamel refrigerator drawer. A Bakelite handle? But of course!

MAKE IT
PAGE 194

Solidifying a game plan before pitching your tents is a rock-solid idea. First off, determine what type of activities will be on your family's camp agenda. Do you enjoy horseshoes, a little bocce ball, or are arts and crafts more up your alley? While roughing out your curriculum, don't forget the basics: three squares a day, campfire songs and roasted marshmallows, and a place to tuck in for the night.

TENTS FOR TOTS

Take it from two moms: Two tots, two tents says ta ta to tussles. All the kiddie campers we know like to have a lean-to of their own, as long as it's not too far away to reach out and touch someone they love. Get them involved from the get-go by letting them design their own sleeping quarters with their favorite junk, and lights-out will be a breeze. Rising to revelry? Hmm, not so much.

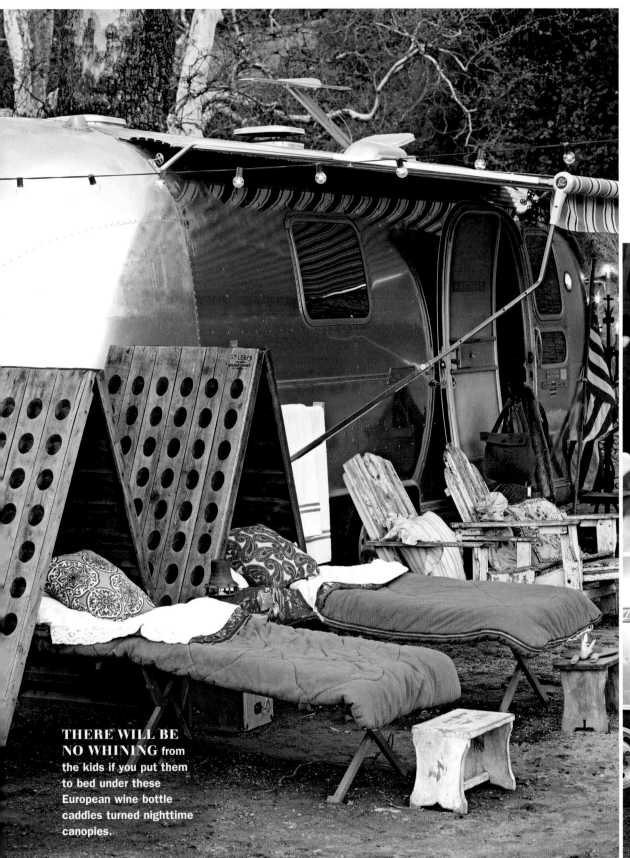

THERE WILL BE NO WHINING from the kids if you put them to bed under these European wine bottle caddies turned nighttime canopies.

BELOW What to do with a train case? Tip it on end and top it with a weighty candleholder that's windproof and kidproof.

BOTTOM If you find yourself a little tight on space, park the coats and other goodies outside the side door.

TOP RIGHT Refrigerator enamelware is oblivious to cold and moisture, making it perfect for use in the great outdrawers.

RIGHT This is a newfangled junk version of an age-old idea. Rope up the flip side of a picnic table and sleep on it. You'll feel better in the morning.

BELOW Encampment never felt so good. From the a.m. to the p.m., this outdoor pad is picture-perfect for family festivities.

WHAT'S IN YOUR CARPET BAG?

Once you have the kids' barracks in order, don't forget to make plans for your own bunkhouse. We were thinking a little bit rustic and a little bit dreamy with this outdoor bedchamber. It's a win-win scenario for Mom and Dad. The crisp white vintage sheets from the linen closet and the age-old sleeping bag from the garage are good examples of finding the middle ground without compromise.

The picnic-table rope bed under a canopy of garden-variety burlap all lit up with ambient glow from a fancy vintage floor lamp follows the same theme. We think Mary Poppins would find this room to be supercalifragilisticexpialidocious.

OLD GLORY GIVES THE nod to this camp-style outdoor bedroom that symbolizes the great American dream. Time for taps!

MIDDAY SNOOZE

IT IS ABSOLUTELY UNDENIABLE: Everybody loves a nap. Snoozing while the sun is high in the sky seems like an extra-special sleep treat. Some may say catnapping even feels a bit mischievous. Almost like short-sheeting someone's bed—sure is fun, but you don't want to get caught. Nonsense!

We're here to give you a few tips to help your wayward self find its way out of work and right into a hammock. Pick out a quiet, secluded, and low-traffic part of your property and get cracking. You'll need a wall to hide behind, a hammock, a table for edibles, and some reading materials to send you off into the world of daydreams. We do have to warn you of one harsh reality before you drift off. You can't really dream away yard work. Unfortunately, it will still be there when you wake up.

RIGHT Tools of the cooking and carpentry trades come together to make one finely chiseled wind chime.

SPREAD THE WORD.
Wilbur has been put into
contemporary confinement
at the workhouse for
noontime nappers. His
crime? Mowing evasion.

No outdoor retreat is complete without some of the comforts found inside the home. The trick is to pick stuff that is rough and tough enough to withstand the elements Mother Nature dishes out. Metal, cement, heavy glass, and wood that's already a little on the warped side are all good choices for dealing with inclement weather conditions.

STICKS AND STONES

You never want to make an outdoor room feel as if you were still inside. There would be no fun in that, so don't stop with just junk furniture and accessories. Go ahead and mix in some bits, pieces, and objects found in nature. We know they can deal with the likes of rain and wind. Incorporating broken branches, rocks, and living greenery into an open-air area keeps it real.

ABOVE After harvesting fruit all day, this weary apple picker takes respite upon a rake handle and provides light to the hammock dwellers.

RIGHT This belt may not have been a big deal to its previous owner, but it provided the perfect punch for this pillow.

FAR RIGHT Do you have any dead branches left behind from last year's fall cleanup? Lace them up with rope and corral your magazines.

PARTICIPATING IN A
nap can leave a person parched.
An old tabletop supported by
salvaged cast-iron legs holds
treats for the tuckered.

RIGHT Save the radials from the landfill and build yourself a rubber privacy wall. You wouldn't want the neighbors catching you napping.

BELOW This urine collection bottle is what they call "new" old stock: purchased, but never used. Or at least that's what they told us.

KNOW-HOW

Keep an open mind when it comes to ugly trash. With a little ingenuity, just about anything can be made useful again, particularly in outdoor spaces. Old car tires are just one good example. Next time you pass by a salvage yard, stop in and have a peek. You may just surprise yourself with what you uncover.

TIRE(D) OF THE SAME OLD THING?

This outdoor corner is a fine example of the JUNKMARKET mantra: Save the earth one piece of junk at a time. We love all kinds of junk, but the stuff that's headed for the city dump reigns supreme on our list.

Here we collected quite a number of these unmentionables and put them together to create an outdoor sanctuary that gives new meaning to the phrase "trash to treasure." The wall built from tires laid the rubber foundation for our junky plan. A tabletop pulled from the burn pile, a rusty garden gate, and some typical junk fare like Mason jars put the icing on the bare treads.

MAKE IT
PAGE 195

LEFT Old tools like these chisels are really pieces of art. Take them out of the garage and enjoy their soothing sounds.

BELOW Flowers planted in an earthenware bowl and placed in a garden étagère lend a sense of softness to this industrial catnap corner.

Incorporating junk into your tabletop décor does not mean you can't be living stylishly large. It's quite the contrary. Working with *objet d'junk* actually gives you more freedom to be you and helps you to establish a setting that will look like no other. You know how embarrassing it can be when you show up at a party in the same dress as someone else. Well, we don't want that to happen at home, either.

SALVAGED SMORGASBORD

Junk can come from many different places, not just flea markets. To get this table all junked up, we found ourselves in many junk haunts. An army-surplus store, an antique mall, a used-restaurant-supply store, and, yes, even a used-medical-supply place all provided pieces to this puzzle. Remember, the hunt is half the fun!

ABOVE If you have a space lacking in greenery, you can always spruce things up a bit with a bouquet of fresh tulips.

BELOW These napkins are kept shipshape in napkin rings that once buckled the belt of a United States naval officer.

After working with Sue for only a day, Georgia found it necessary to put her in a rubber room.

JUNK ABOUNDS at this snack station. Jar candleholders, a baker's tool tulip vase, and— heavens to Betsy, what's holding the lemonade?

A RED CHICKEN COOP that was adorable from the outside needed some tender-loving care on the inside. Found space right at your back door: what a treat!

Rooms to Bloom

What would the world be without beautiful rooms that go bloom? We think pretty darn drab, dreary, and oh-so-boring. Junkers are anything but dull, so we went in search of outdoor spaces that were in desperate need of some junk-style green thumb know-how.

From the serenity of a greenhouse made for meditation to the funky sounds of the sea-splashin' junk band, you'll be sure to find more than a few take-to-heart ideas while leafing through the pages of this blooming chapter. Have fun, and may the hands of Helga, our happy mannequin, shed green goodness upon yours.

Spice up your herb garden with some garden markers planted in colorful old spools.

SWEET POTTING SHED

A N ABANDONED CHICKEN coop could remain just that, but why waste a perfectly good space and lose out on the potential to create a pretty and posh potting shed? Now there's a tongue twister for you! Say that three times, we dare you. Moving right along, you can see by taking a quick peek through these chicken-wire doors that the original floors and walls of the coop were left rustic and exposed. This was done intentionally because a room for potting is bound to get dirty, so no need to fuss about all that.

The fun was introducing fresh, fancy, and feminine junk touches to this otherwise pastoral interior. We brightened up the traditional farmhouse red, green, and white color scheme to turn a once-withering dark, dank corner into a bright and junk-beautiful place to pot. While we were at it, we decided to throw in, free of charge, a place to plant your own self. A puffy chair and a crusty table provide the place to plop and plot your next garden.

BELOW Planting flowers in a wee little urinal will put a smile on your face every time you enter your garden shed. It's a fact.

BOTTOM Keep a good supply of vintage hardware on hand. These handy-dandy shed hooks are ideal for aprons and other potting props.

THE USE OF BRIGHT white wicker and wood help to make this plant-processing place brighter, happier, and more vibrant.

ABOVE A potting table should put everything you need at your fingertips. This vintage two-tiered model with a lower shelf does just that.

Behind wire for egg nabbing, Sue uses her one phone call to make bail.

The main attraction in a workroom for blooms is the indispensable potting table. This baby will be your command post from the time the snow melts until you put your last flower to bed in the fall. Keeping this in mind, choose a location within your shed that is conducive to the hours of soil toil that lie ahead. This hen pen had only one set of windows, so the positioning decision of our potter's bench was obvious. We all suffer enough light deprivation throughout the winter months.

WHAT'S ON YOUR TABLE?

Potting sheds tend to be smallish but need to perform a big function. Make the most of the space you have by setting a table that will address all of your needs. Planting, transplanting, sprouting seedlings, staking, and tying are just a few of the tasks you will need to consider when setting up shop. Take the time to design, and you'll be a glad-handed gardener.

BELOW LEFT This henhouse regular decided not to fly the coop. A metal chick transporter now carries seedlings to the garden.

BELOW These windows are architectural masterpieces and add a touch of unanticipated sophistication to this down-home décor.

MAKE YOUR GARDEN shack work for you. Include a place where you can plan your plantings. Warning! You may have to fight Whiskers for the chair.

GOODIES GALORE!

Knowing that you will be up close and personal with your potting shed throughout the growing season, you may just as well make it a pleasant place to be. How do you achieve pretty and practical? Very simple, friends! Organize your thoughts, your needs, and your wishes and put them to paper.

Start by shopping your garage and other at-home storage closets to gather items on your gardening list. You'll be amazed at what those cargo closets have to offer. An out-of-commission chair, wobbly tables, dilapidated ladders, and cast-aside containers no longer good enough for indoor use will thrive again in the shack for showing. After collecting all of the stuff you need to contain, house, or store them, head off to your local garden center and procure the necessary supplies and plants that will bring your gardens into full-flowering splendor.

ABOVE **Love these! Commonplace yet beautiful glass chicken-watering devices are ideal for holding bulbs and other gardening necessities.**

LEFT **Do you own a rickety cool stool with top issues? If so, feel free to flip it upside down and add a glass top. Problem solved!**

FAR LEFT **Tote your seeds with ease with this sweet and simple caddy. The blue Mason jars are lined with seed packets for easy identification.**

A PAIR OF SHUTTERS with cottage-style cutouts were called to task to make a supply shelf for a neglected and out-of-use outbuilding. A trip to the hardware store, a can of spray paint, and a set of beginner tools will unleash the inner junk builder in you on this one.

MATERIALS NEEDED

- 2 shutters
- Spray paint
- Natural rope
- 4 eye hooks
- 4 clamp bolts
- 2 springs
- 3 old hooks
- Vintage or new paper towel holder
- 3 wood screws (1½ in.)

TOOLS NEEDED

- Junker's Toolbox (see p. 181).

METHOD

1 Spray-paint the shutters white and let dry. Ⓐ

2 Attach the shutters using wood screws, forming an "L." An extra set of hands will come in handy here.

3 Predrill holes for large eye hooks on the top edge of the shelf back and the bottom edge of the shelf bottom.

4 Using a screwdriver, twist the eye hooks into the drilled holes. Ⓑ

5 Measure and cut lengths of rope to thread through the eye hooks and secure the shelf.

6 At the bottom of the shelf, thread the cut rope through the eye hook and secure using a clamp bolt and needle-nose pliers. Ⓒ

7 Slide a spring onto the rope on each side of the shelf. Ⓓ

8 Thread the rope through the eye hook at the top of the shelf and secure in the same manner as above. Keep the tension tight to support the shelf.

9 Mark locations for the paper towel holder and hooks on the underside of the shelf and predrill holes to size. Attach the paper towel holder with ¼-in. screws.

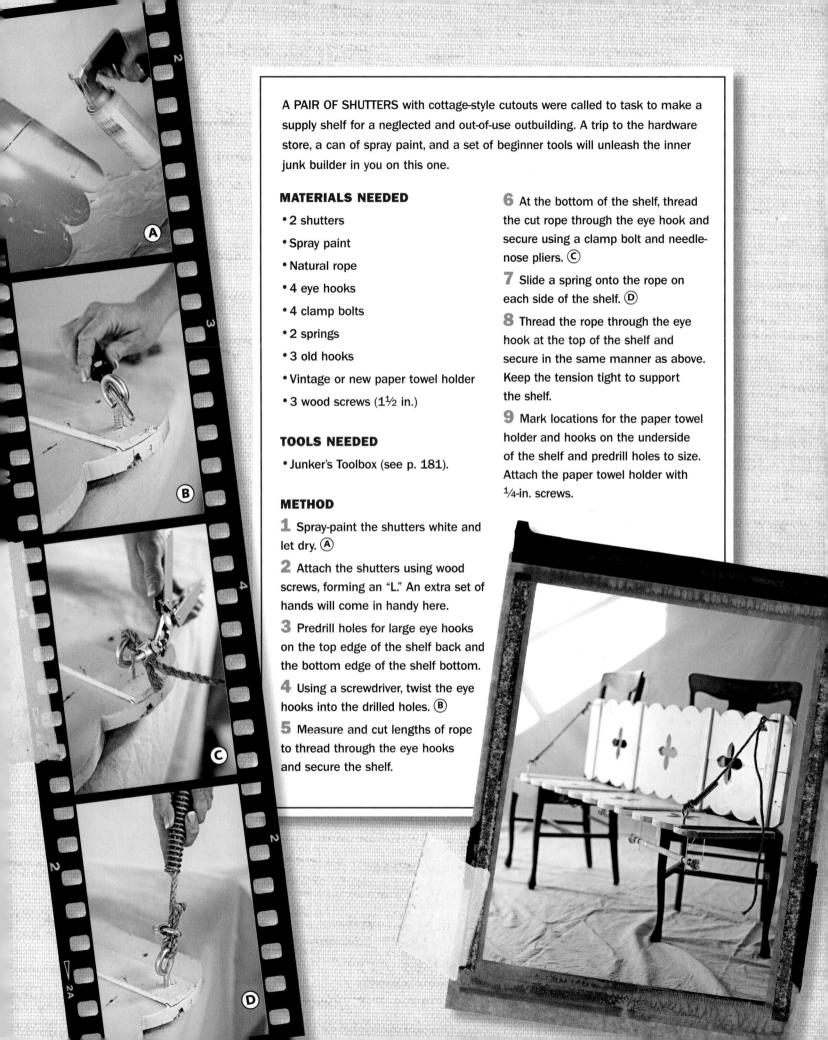

SEASIDE GARDEN

A DRIFTWOOD TALE that's fully equipped for tending container gardens will make your job a walk on the beach.

FASTEN YOUR SEAT BELTS, because waves of creativity are about to come crashing in your direction. We've addressed different strokes for different folks before, and this is one of the style files we go gaga over. Due to the ruthless reality that life is so serious much of the time, we adore planning places that offer up a sense of humor and a sense of style to match. This seaside locale presented us with the ultimate panorama to kick up our junk heels and have some good old-fashioned fun.

As you can see, we pulled our color palette from the vista surrounding the oceanside deck. From there, it was anything goes. Some of the junk has a nautical background, but much of it seemed like it fell from the sky and landed in the place it was meant to be. The fun has just begun. So say hello to Helga's house and watch the deck as playful personalities unfold.

Sue's next book? Motel Planting for Dummies. Sure to be a best seller!

MAKE IT
PAGE 196

LEFT Hands from glove factories can be found just about anywhere you find junk.

ABOVE A small table and small patio plants require a small planting pad. One hot-water bottle coming right up!

LEFT On an ordinary day, we may have passed our eight-tentacled friend by, but for this pad? Most certainly not!

BELOW Hilarious Helga poses for her Hollywood glam shot in some cool new shades. Sizzlin' hot, Helga.

BOTTOM If you don't have a hose nearby, sport one of these on your deck. Fill, tip, and water. No heavy lifting involved.

HELGA RULES

A plain vanilla deck and hot tub area come to life through the incorporation of playful party-time pieces and pals. Ocean blue scaffolding got the beach ball rolling by providing some lines in the sand, at least partially sheltering views of the in-the-laptop neighbor. Hanging plants and metal buoys offered even more privacy. Just a handful of furniture was needed, and a only a few garden essentials were required to complete the hot tub platform décor.

If you saw these junky items separately, you might not have guessed that they would act as such a finely synchronized team, but lo and behold, they work. And then, of course, there's Helga standing watch over the impending festivities in her vintage bathing suit (c. 1942) and bathing cap (c. 1952). Looks like her umbrella could use some repair.

ABOVE Are you looking for a way to define a space and hold some bloomin' goods? Scaffolding held firm in sand buckets just may be your answer.

RIGHT A once-oceanbound bouncing buoy now sails in the breeze and adds nautical flavor to an oceanside retreat.

RIGHT The beauty and the beast: A metal toolbox is just right as a planter for a patio-perfect and herbalicious garden.

BELOW It's time to rinse and spit. Oops, that was in the old days. A reworked dental bowl is all hosed up and ready to water the plants.

KNOW-HOW

Purchasing quirky junk can be a little tricky. There is a fine line between fanciful junk and junk that's just plain bad. Yep, you heard it here: Some things should just remain where they are, in your memory banks. If you are a fun junk-seeking shopper, it's best to have a decorating theme. Then your finds will look intentional, not silly.

SWAP! YOU'RE IT!

This deck is not all play and no work. Shootie doots! Oh well, if there's a job to be done, it's not so bad in a place like this. Let's face it, the view is spectacular and the tools are worthy of a slap-happy grin or two. The only things you have to be concerned about are the seagulls flying overhead. We highly recommend gardening hats with wide brims. Experience is the best teacher.

The shiny and new surface of the deck gave plenty of leeway when it came to applying the junkmasters' touch. A nearby true-to-the-core swap meet coffered the sweet and sassy junk we were looking for. A quick roundabout at the meet and an almost embarrassingly small amount of coin spent, and we were good to go. Drive-by junking: It's the only way.

ABOVE **Gauges are graphic and cool. Pair one with some tried-and-true minnow bucket planters for a look that's overboard with style.**

BELOW LEFT **Don't fret about the mad dentist and the dreadful drill. It's all good. The only thing gone mad here is the watering brigade.**

Funny, Sue's never around when there's heavy lifting to do. Call it a junker's sixth sense.

MEDITATION GARDEN

A GREENHOUSE attached to your home provides yearlong radiant sunshine and warmth. Consider this addition next time you're in the market.

RELAXATION—WE ALL want it, we all need it, but most of the time, we just dream about it. Gaze thoughtfully into this lush greenhouse meditation garden, take in the peaceful surroundings, and wrap your arms around the notion that what you have been longing for can become a reality.

Our inspiration for this project was the room-length, table-height adult sandbox. The box was intended for potting and drainage, but once we started playing in the sand, we realized it possessed a pure and natural healing quality.

The room was fairly barren when we found it, and we decided the simplicity of the space was what we were drawn to. Our mission was to move it from the manufacturing park to the Zen zone while maintaining its austere look and feel. This time it was not about blooming buds, but about different shades of green. A wide variety of greenery, including topiaries from rosemary to scented geraniums, were employed to give a fresh fragrance to the garden. To complement the plant life, we chose junk extras with a combination of industrial, rustic, and natural undertones.

ABOVE **A crumbling yet sturdy hollow concrete column base gives a potted plant a lift. It's elegant and functional, a crafty combination.**

RIGHT **A candlelit vintage miner's lantern will help you stay in the zone while tending to your sand garden.**

ABOVE Use a shower-head with many holes to make hanging a breeze. Old upholstery tacks fit snugly into holes to hold chime-bearing twine.

RIGHT This vintage showerhead has seen better days—or has it? Dress it up with twine and bamboo, and you have yourself a soothing wind chime.

BOTTOM RIGHT A weather-beaten spire attached to a support beam becomes a thing of beauty once again, and it's a plant hanger. Beat that!

LEAN AND GREEN

This long, narrow room needed an end point separating it from the rest of the space to allow for quiet reflection—in other words, creating a barrier isolating you from the less enlightened. Ha! A wall of green combined with old-world garden accoutrement seemed the obvious choice. We went in search of terra-cotta pots à la crusty to house most of the plants.

To build the wall, we stacked the greens on the floor and on the table, and we hung some from the ceiling, creating depth and interest. Bare garden trellises and cement pots were also added for intrigue. Our favorite is the curved iron grate with the flickering candle beyond. All of these elements rolled up into one ball of gardening twine will get you what you came for: a little peace and quiet. Finally!

GREEN PLANTS
all done up in mossy
terra-cotta, well-worn
concrete, and rusty
metal fit this space like
a gardener's glove.

TAKE YOUR MEDITATION

A place to ponder should be clean and simple, but not necessarily void of eye candy. Whoa, that may make you fall asleep rather than reach a higher state of consciousness. We definitely would not want that. There is a way to achieve a "somebody lives here" look without overclutter.

To stay within the style of the greenhouse framework, we incorporated galvanized metal pieces, architectural remnants, and some very graphic elements. You might also notice that there are many circular shapes built in, symbolizing infinity, completeness, and wholeness. Now there's some deep thought from a junker!

But, seriously, there is something about the sphere that says everything is right

with the world, at least for today. Slip a circle on for size, and you'll see what we mean. Also, to avoid the pesky clutter bug, follow one simple rule of the green thumb. Items should not only be easy on the eyes, but they should also perform a function. Adhering to this tenet will help you select your junkables wisely and wipe out the insect population without the use of harmful pesticides.

ABOVE **You'll need a way to tend to all these living things. Carve out room for a station that houses all the tools of the trade.**

LEFT **This funky metal outdoor hose thingy said, "Please, let me hold the twine and wire. Can I, can I, oh pretty please?" Some things are just meant to be.**

JUNK GEMS

1. Bamboo cut to size meets modern drawer pulls to form an industrial wind chime for your listening enjoyment.

2. Keep plenty of stones for your Zen garden close at hand. Ours take their place atop a step from an old buggy.

3. A sifter of sorts and a root beer cork join forces to become a one-of-a-kind caddy for your smaller gardening implements.

4. A Zen day without incense is like a day without sunshine. The smaller holes in the organ pipe holder are perfect for the stick variety.

5. Here's what we're talking about. A simple, round 12-lb. shot put speaks volumes when it comes to style.

6. The exposed pipes throughout the greenhouse helped us to define our designing course of action for meditation perfection.

Ambient lighting is a requirement for those in the know when it comes to meditation. An organ pipe holder makes for a great place to sit the candles.

ABOVE **Move mini oil cans about in the sand of your Zen garden with the same precision as chess pieces without fear of checkmate.**

LEFT **Our selection of smalls includes stones, oil cans, and forks, but set your imagination free and come up with your own sand pieces.**

NATURE CALLS

Our hand-crafted-from-junk Zen garden is the center of this universe. A full-service meditation station is not complete without one. We know you've all seen them at novelty stores and healthy living retail outlets, but we thought a handmade variety would be even better. Reflection hour is a very personal thing, and we believe your garden to rake should echo your individual creativity and state of mind. While mapping out your room to ruminate, set the stage with the Z-garden and then add pieces that will enhance your existential experience.

Take plenty of time here; there's no need to rush through this part of the process. This portion of your space is of utmost importance if you are truly searching for a place to let it all go for an hour or so. Once all of your players are chosen, the movement of the silky sand and the feel of smooth stones will put you right where you want to be—in the zone.

MAKE IT
PAGE 197

ALL PUT TOGETHER and tied up with twine, this tranquil space has much to offer. Sand, rocks, and breeze are all present and accounted for. The only thing missing is rain.

How to Make the Rest

Disclaimer: The junk items used in our projects may be one-of-a-kind items. The instructions on these pages refer only to how we transformed the junk we found. You may need to improvise to achieve your desired transformation—and chances are, your stuff will look even better.

Sue's patio tables turned out wheelly well.

Junker's Toolbox

- Drill
- Assorted Drill Bits for metal and wood
- Screwdriver
- Hammer
- Wood Saw
- Metal Saw
- Miter Saw
- Pliers (straight and needle-nose)
- Tape Measure
- Straightedge
- Marker
- Bolt Cutter
- Heavy Wire Cutter
- Tin Snips
- Scissors
- Pry Bar
- Paint Brushes
- Sanding Blocks or Paper

Please Enter

HVAC Decorative Garden Stake

MATERIALS NEEDED

- Assorted HVAC parts
- Threaded rod of desired height (ours was 3 ft. by $\frac{5}{16}$ in.)
- Washers and nuts to fit the threaded rod
- Old outdoor faucet handles

TOOLS NEEDED

- Junker's Toolbox (see p. 181)

METHOD

1 Bend down the flanged edges of the HVAC tube to resemble flower petals.

2 Thread the rod through the existing holes that are on the sides of the HVAC tube. Ⓐ

3 Secure the threaded rod to the HVAC tube with a washer and a nut. We used #10 size. Ⓑ

4 Attach an old faucet handle to the threaded rod in the center of the flower with metal wire. Trim and curl the ends of the wire. Ⓒ

p. 7

Frame and Drawer Window Box

MATERIALS NEEDED

- Vintage or new frame
- Old drawer
- Bead-board paneling
- Paint
- Vintage letters and numbers
- Moss and flowers
- Eye hooks for hanging
- Screws

TOOLS NEEDED

- Junker's Toolbox (see p. 181)
- Gorilla Glue

METHOD

1 Measure and cut the bead-board paneling to fit inside the frame.

2 Paint the bead-board and let dry.

3 Using Gorilla Glue, adhere the bead board to inset of the frame. Tip: A little goes a long way, so use sparingly. Ⓐ

4 With a wood saw, carefully saw off the back of the old drawer to the desired depth. (Ours was 10 in.) Ⓑ

5 Attach the drawer to the framed bead-board from the back, using screws. Pre-drilling is helpful so the drawer doesn't split or crack.

6 Attach the numbers and letters to the bead-board and drawer front with Gorilla Glue.

7 Plant the drawer with your favorite posies.

8 Hang with eye hooks twisted into top of the frame.

p. 10

Ⓐ

Ⓑ

p. 24

Vintage Grate Door Wreath

MATERIALS NEEDED

- Pre-made evergreen wreath
- Vintage grate
- Assorted floral leaves and greens
- Florist's wire

TOOLS NEEDED

- Junker's Toolbox (see p. 181)

METHOD

1 Place the vintage round grate on top of the wreath, in the center.

2 Wire the grate onto the wreath with florist's wire. (A)

3 Wire the assorted florals together with the florist's wire. (B)

4 Turn the wreath over and, with the florals placed in the desired location on the grate, wire them to both the wreath and grate. (C)

Ⓐ

Ⓑ

Ⓒ

Patio Perfection

Rain Barrel Umbrella Stand

MATERIALS NEEDED

- Galvanized rain barrel or other barrel
- 2 wine cask tops or wooden disks, approximately 24 in. round
- 6 L-brackets
- Screws
- Coupling
- Umbrella

TOOLS NEEDED

- Junker's Toolbox (see p. 181)

METHOD

1 Working on the inside of the rain barrel, attach a coupling with screws to the center bottom of the barrel. Ⓐ

2 Attach one wine cask top or wooden disc to the bottom of the rain barrel using 3 "L" brackets and screws.

3 Drill a hole in the center of the other wine cask top with a drill to accommodate your umbrella. (Ours was 1¾ in.) Ⓑ

4 Attach the pre-drilled wine cask to the top of the barrel with the 3 remaining "L" brackets. Ⓒ

5 Stand upright and insert your umbrella.

Ⓐ

Ⓑ

Ⓒ

p. 28

Spiffed-Up Spool Table

MATERIALS NEEDED

- Large electrical spool
- 30 washers (we used $5/16$ in. by $1\frac{1}{4}$ in.)
- 30 self-drilling screws (we used #14 by $\frac{3}{4}$ in.)
- Twine
- Lightweight quilting fabric (4 different patterns)
- Mod Podge®
- Lazy Susan hardware to fit the top of the spool and accommodate your tray (ours was 6 in. by 6 in.)
- Old or new round metal tray (ours was 12 in.)
- Gorilla Super Glue

TOOLS NEEDED

- Junker's Toolbox (see p. 181)
- 2-in. sponge brush
- Hex drill bit for screws
- Spray bottle with water

METHOD

1 Remove a few wooden slats from the sides of the spool. This will make step #3 so much easier as it will give you room to work.

2 Cut strips of fabric to the approximate length and width of each wooden slat.

3 Adhere the fabric to the slats with Mod Podge using a sponge brush. Wet sand lightly when dry for a smooth finish. Ⓐ

4 Replace the slats you previously removed and tap into place with a hammer or mallet.

5 Add washers and screws to the slats midway between the top and bottom.

6 Evenly space the screws and drill them into the side of the top of the spool through the washers.

7 Wrap the twine around the screws, behind the washers, to create an "over-under" pattern. Ⓑ

8 Place the lazy Susan hardware on top of the spool and adhere with screws. Ⓒ

9 Attach the metal tray to the lazy Susan using Gorilla Super Glue.

p. 38

Porches with Panache

Enamel Pot Planters

p. 60

MATERIALS NEEDED

- Vintage enameled teapots
- 4 vintage drawer knobs for each teapot
- Nuts to fit knobs
- Vintage salt spoons
- Assorted flowers
- Twine

TOOLS NEEDED

- Junker's Toolbox (see p. 181)

METHOD

1 Drill a few holes in the bottom of the teapot for drainage. Ⓐ

2 Measure and drill holes in the bottom of the teapot for the knob feet.

3 Attach the feet through the bottom and secure with a nut. Ⓑ

4 Drill two small holes in the side of the pot and run twine through the holes from the back. Tie twine around the spoons to secure. Ⓒ

5 Plant your favorite posies in the pot.

Backyard Bliss

p. 70

Fairy Garden

MATERIALS NEEDED

- Vintage wooden crate (ours was 6 in. deep)
- Assorted stones for feet
- An assortment of ground cover plants
- Fairy (we used a vintage toy top, a vintage sewing kit, and vintage hat pins)
- Vintage dollhouse toy
- Vintage Jell-O molds
- Vintage jewelry
- Magnifying glass

TOOLS NEEDED

- Junker's Toolbox (see p. 181)
- Gorilla Glue

METHOD

1 Drill holes in the bottom of the crate for drainage. Ⓐ

2 Attach stones to the corners of the crate with Gorilla Glue. Remember, a little goes a long way! Ⓑ

3 Flip the crate over when it's dry and fill with ground cover and plants. Ⓒ

4 To make the fairy, we used a child's toy top and gave her a hat made from felt in a vintage sewing kit. Her wings are hat pins.

5 Design a room for your fairy. Use your imagination here and enlist the help of your little ones! We used Jell-O molds, dollhouse furniture, old toys, and vintage jewelry. And just so you don't miss a fairy moment we included a vintage magnifying glass.

Tripod Torch

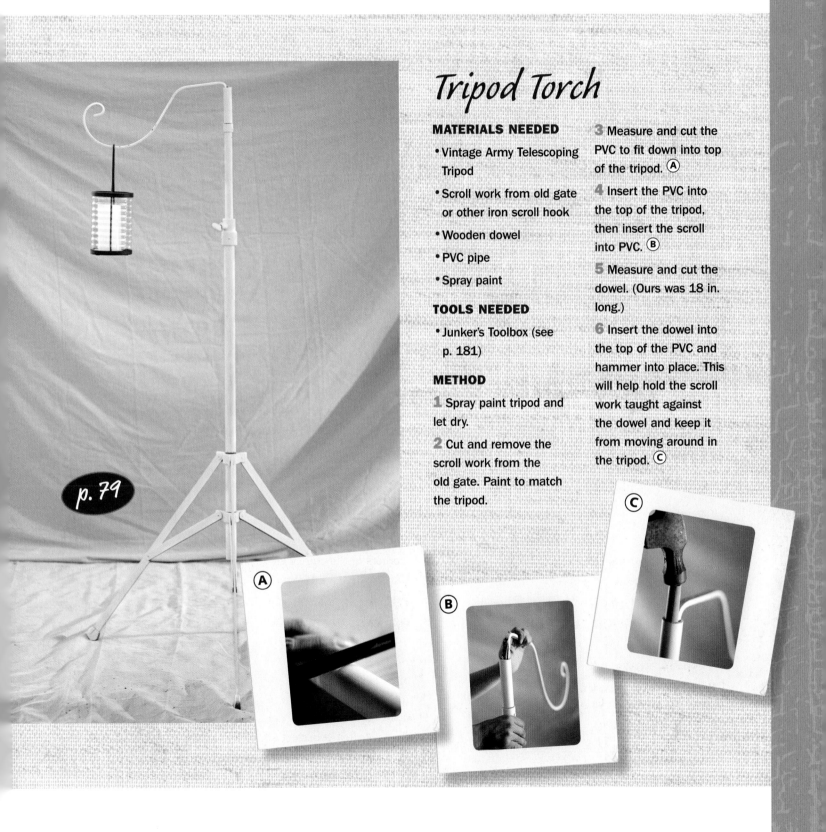

MATERIALS NEEDED

- Vintage Army Telescoping Tripod
- Scroll work from old gate or other iron scroll hook
- Wooden dowel
- PVC pipe
- Spray paint

TOOLS NEEDED

- Junker's Toolbox (see p. 181)

METHOD

1 Spray paint tripod and let dry.

2 Cut and remove the scroll work from the old gate. Paint to match the tripod.

3 Measure and cut the PVC to fit down into top of the tripod. Ⓐ

4 Insert the PVC into the top of the tripod, then insert the scroll into PVC. Ⓑ

5 Measure and cut the dowel. (Ours was 18 in. long.)

6 Insert the dowel into the top of the PVC and hammer into place. This will help hold the scroll work taught against the dowel and keep it from moving around in the tripod. Ⓒ

p. 79

Cooking Out

Scaffolding Buffet

MATERIALS NEEDED

- Vintage scaffolding
- Wooden boards to fit inside scaffolding (ours were 1 in. by 12 in.)
- Vintage towel racks
- Conduit clamps
- Spray paint
- Medium-colored pine stain
- Screws

TOOLS NEEDED

- Junker's Toolbox (see p. 181)

METHOD

1 Paint the scaffolding and let dry. Ⓐ

2 Measure and cut the boards to fit desired length. (Ours were 6 ft.) Ⓑ

3 Apply stain to the boards. Let dry. Ⓒ

4 Slide the two boards onto the scaffolding and secure from underneath with a conduit clamp. Ⓓ

5 Mark placement for the towel holders and pre-drill holes. Using a screwdriver, screw the towel holders into place.

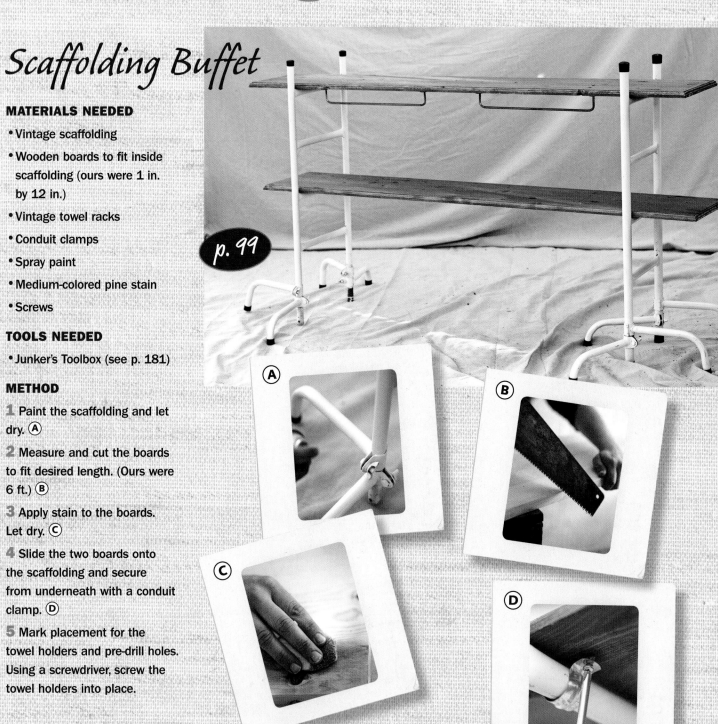

p. 99

Ⓐ Ⓑ Ⓒ Ⓓ

Skateboard/Stirrup Towel Holder

MATERIALS NEEDED

- Vintage skateboard
- Vintage stirrup
- Screws
- Manila rope

TOOLS NEEDED

- Junker's Toolbox (see p. 181)
- Skidmore's Woodfinish Cleaner

METHOD

1 Clean up the skateboard with a coat of Skidmore's Woodfinish Cleaner.

2 Measure and mark for holes at the top of the skateboard.

3 Drill the holes where marked with a ¼-in. bit. Ⓐ

4 Cut a length of rope to hang the skateboard. (Ours was 30 in.)

5 Thread the rope through the holes, from back, and knot. Ⓑ

6 Lay the stirrup on the skateboard and mark the top for screws.

7 Attach the screws at the marks with screwdriver, leaving them extended out to support the stirrup. Ⓒ

p. 106

Dining al Fresco

Button Board Tray

MATERIALS NEEDED

- Vintage drawer or other shallow drawer
- Vintage drawer pulls
- Vintage button board
- Decorative paper
- Ribbon
- Upholstery tacks
- Plexiglas®
- Screws

TOOLS NEEDED

- Junker's Toolbox (see p. 181)
- X-Acto® roller-style cutter
- Spray adhesive
- Gorilla Super Glue

METHOD

1 Measure and cut paper to fit inside the drawer.

2 Adhere the paper to the inside of the drawer using a spray adhesive. Ⓐ

3 Attach vintage drawer pulls to the ends of the drawer using screws and a screwdriver. You may want to pre-drill the holes. Ⓑ

4 Place the button board on top of the paper and adhere with spray adhesive.

5 Measure and cut the ribbon to frame the button board.

6 Use upholstery tacks to keep the ribbon in place.

Tip: A drop of Gorilla Super Glue under each tack helps keep things in place.

7 Place one screw inside each corner of the tray, through the paper, and screw in slightly.

8 Measure and cut the Plexiglas to fit inside the drawer using an X-acto blade. If this task is too difficult you can have the hardware store cut the Plexiglas when you purchase it. Ⓒ

9 Slide Plexiglas inside the drawer and rest it on the screws.

Ⓐ

Ⓑ

Ⓒ

p. 123

p. 129

Wagon Picnic Table

MATERIALS NEEDED

- Vintage child's wagon
- 2 old wooden folding tables
- 4 hinges
- Screws and nuts (they may come with the hinges)
- Slide bolt lock set
- Skidmore's Woodfinish Cleaner

TOOLS NEEDED

- Junker's Toolbox (see p. 181)

METHOD

1 With a screwdriver, remove the bases from the folding tables.

2 Clean the tabletops with Skidmore's Woodfinish Cleaner. Ⓐ

3 Place the hinges on the ends of the wagon and tabletops and mark the holes. You want the hinges on the ends so the top opens in the center of the wagon.

4 Drill the marked locations. It may be helpful to remove the tops and end pieces of the wagon to do this.

5 Attach the hinges with the screws and nuts using needlenose pliers. Ⓑ

6 Once both the tabletops are secured, lay out the lock hardware on the center where the tables meet and attach the lock mechanism using a screwdriver. Ⓒ

Ⓐ

Ⓑ

Ⓒ

Sleeping

Cod Pole Frame

MATERIALS NEEDED

- Vintage cod fishing poles
- Carriage bolts and nuts (ours were $3/8$ in.)
- Hollow metal tubing
- Vintage ruler (optional)
- Old or new photos

TOOLS NEEDED

- Junker's Toolbox (see p. 181)

METHOD

1 Lay photo on top of the cod pole and decide placement. Mark lightly with a pencil.

2 Push a bolt through the pole at each of the marked locations. Ⓐ

3 Secure each bolt with a nut on the back of the line. Ⓑ

4 Tuck photo just under the bolt heads.

5 To make the cod pole stand upright, cut and bend a length of hollow metal tubing to form an easel and slide it through the pole on the back. Be careful as the tubing breaks easily. Ⓒ

6 Alternately, use a vintage ruler threaded through the back of the pole to help prop your photo frame.

p. 144

under the Stars

p. 153

Chisel Wind Chime

MATERIALS NEEDED

- Vintage strainer
- 4 vintage chisels or other vintage tools
- 1 vintage drill or other tool for the center of the chime
- Spring to hang the chime
- 4 small screw eye bolts
- 5 larger screw eye bolts and nuts
- Thin rope
- Chain, old or new

TOOLS NEEDED

- Junker's Toolbox (see p. 181)
- Allen wrench (optional)

METHOD

1 Pre-drill holes in the ends of the chisels to accommodate the small screw eyes.

2 Using an Allen wrench or screwdriver twist the screw eyes onto the ends of the chisels. Ⓐ

3 Measure and cut lengths of rope and tie them to the small screw eyes on the chisels and to the vintage drill or other tool. Vary the lengths of the rope for a fun look. (Our center tool, the vintage drill, was hung at 20 in.)

4 Tie the other ends of the ropes to the large screw eyes.

5 Thread the large screw eye bolts through the mesh on the strainer and secure with a nut. Be sure to spread the weight of the tools evenly or the chime will hang unevenly. Ⓑ

6 Repeat step 5 with the center tool, securing it to the center of the strainer. Ⓒ

7 Measure and cut 4 lengths of chain to hang the chime at the desired height (ours was 14 in.).

8 With needlenose pliers, attach the chains to the legs of the strainer by opening up the end link and closing it around the strainer leg. Ⓓ

9 Hang the chime from the chains attached to the spring at the top.

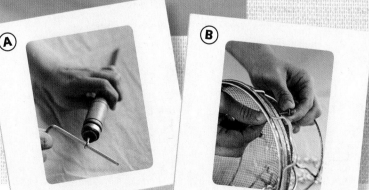

Ⓐ

Ⓑ

Ⓒ

Ⓓ

Rooms to Bloom

Helping Hands

MATERIALS NEEDED

- Vintage glove forms
- Wooden bases from a craft or hobby store
- Wooden dowels
- Scrabble® letters to spell "Helping Hands"
- Medium wood stain

TOOLS NEEDED

- Junker's Toolbox (see p. 181)
- Gorilla Glue

METHOD

1 Measure and drill holes for two dowels in each wooden base to fit inside the width of the hands. Ⓐ

2 Measure and cut the dowels to fit inside the height of hands.

3 Stain wooden bases and let dry.

4 Push the dowels into the pre-drilled holes and secure with Gorilla Glue or wood-swelling glue. Let dry.

Remember to use the glue sparingly as it expands. Ⓑ

5 Using Gorilla Glue, attach Scrabble letters to spell "Helping" on one base and "Hands" on the other. Ⓒ

6 When dowels and letters are dry, slide hands down over dowels to secure.

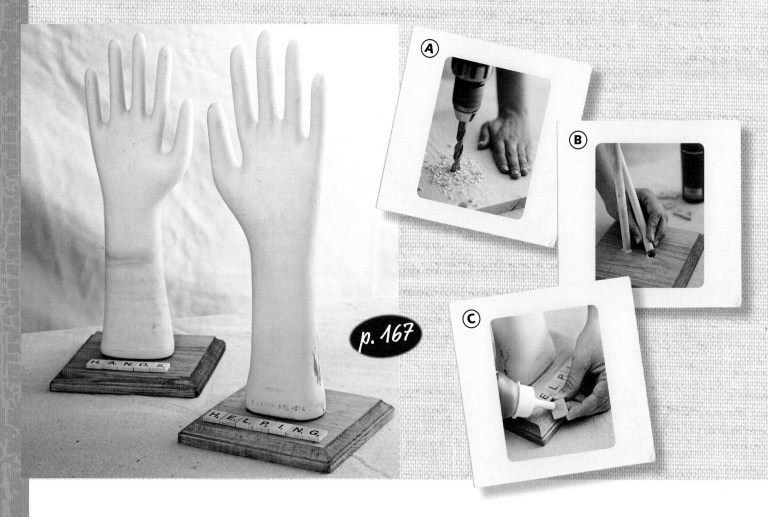

p. 167

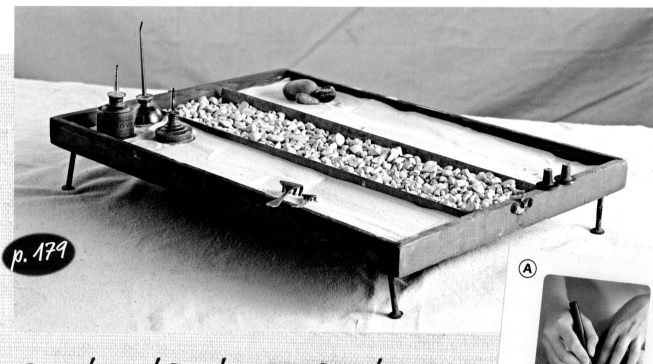

p. 179

Sand and Rock Zen Garden

MATERIALS NEEDED

- Vintage seed separator or other shallow vintage drawer with dividers
- 4 vintage railroad nails
- Roll of cork
- Silica sand or other fine-grain sand
- Polished stones
- Vintage fork
- Vintage baby oil cans

TOOLS NEEDED

- Junker's Toolbox (see p. 181)
- Gorilla Tape

METHOD

1 Measure and cut the cork to fit tightly into the bottom of the drawer. Place the cork in the drawer bottom. Ⓐ

2 Secure the cork using Gorilla Tape on the edges of the cork and up the sides of the drawer, using the tape to frame the cork into the drawer and sealing it so the sand won't sift out.

3 Flip the drawer over and hammer the railroad nails into the bottom four corners of the drawer, making sure to keep them level. Flip the drawer back over. Ⓑ

4 Fill the drawer with sand in the two outside sections and with stones in the center section.

5 With needle-nose pliers, bend the tines of the fork downward to form a mini rake. Ⓒ

6 Place baby oil cans, forks, and large stones on the sand and enjoy your Zen moment.

Resources

A GLANCE INTO THE PAST
401 E. Branch St.
Arroyo Grande, CA 93420
(805) 489-5666

AARDVARK ANTIQUES
126 E. Branch St.
Arroyo Grande, CA 93420
(805) 473-3584

ANTHOLOGY
74 N. Main St.
Templeton, CA 93465
(805) 434-5533

ANTIQUE CENTER MALL
1239 Monterey St.
San Luis Obispo, CA 93401
(805) 541-4040

ARCHITECTURAL ANTIQUES
1330 Quincy St. NE
Minneapolis, MN 55413
(612) 332-8344
www.archantiques.com

AUNTIE M'S ANTIQUES
911 Main St.
Hopkins, MN 55343
(952) 933-1144

THE BUFFALO NICKEL
1004 3rd St. S.
Buffalo, MN 55313
(763) 682-4735
www.buffalonickelantiques.com

**CHAMELEON FABRICS,
FURNITURE AND DESIGN**
415 E. Branch St.
Arroyo Grande, CA 93420
(805) 481-4104

**THE COTTAGE AT
PACIFIC COAST**
Carey Herlihy
2034 Santa Barbara St.
San Luis Obispo, CA 93401
(805) 543-2191

**THE COUNTRY
CAKE CUPBOARD**
491 Willow Dr. N.
Long Lake, MN 55356
(952) 476-0222

D'KORE WELDING
Doug Knoll
Delano, MN 55328
(612) 201-7489

DAYLIGHT GARDENS
1234 Monterey St.
San Luis Obispo, CA 93401
(805) 547-1234

GEORGIA MOON
Georgia Terrell
141 N. 6th St.
Grover Beach, CA 93433
(805) 489-8908
www.georgia-moon.com

HUNT & GATHER
4944 Xerxes Ave. S.
Minneapolis, MN 55410
(612) 455-0250
www.huntandgatherantiques.com

KELLY & KELLY NURSERY
2325 Watertown Rd.
Long Lake, MN 55356
(952) 473-7337

LEANNTIQUES & FRIENDS
6 N. 10th Ave.
Hopkins, MN 55343
(952) 945-9999 or (952) 212-1693
www.leanntiques.com

LOLL DESIGNS
1325 59th Ave. W.
Duluth, MN 55807
Toll Free: (877) 740-3387
Local: (218) 740-3387
FAX: (218) 525-2850
www.lolldesigns.com

LONG LAKE GLASS
2262 County Rd. 24
Hamel, MN 55340
(763) 473-4845

**NATURES NEST ORGANIC
FARM, BED & BREAKFAST**
Cathy Rose
5412 Brighton Ave. S.E.
Montrose, MN 55363
(763) 972-6891
www.naturesnestfarm.com

OLSON'S MARKET
5249 Highway 12
Maple Plain, MN 55359
(763) 479-6222

**PACIFIC COAST
HOME AND GARDEN**
2034 Santa Barbara St.
San Luis Obispo, CA 93401
(805) 543-2191
www.pchgarden.com

PATIO OUTLET
1107 El Camino Real
Arroyo Grande, CA 93420
(805) 489-1412
www.thepatiooutlet.com

**PATTEA TORRENCE
AT OLD EDNA**
1653 Old Price Cyn. Rd.
San Luis Obispo, CA 93401
(805) 544-8062

REMEMBER WHEN
152 N. Ocean Ave.
Cayucos, CA 93430
(805) 995-1232

REMEMBER WHEN TOO
36 N. Ocean Ave.
Cayucos, CA 93430
(805) 995-2074

**RICH MAN-POOR MAN
ANTIQUES MALL**
146 N. Ocean Ave.
Cayucos, CA 93430
(805) 995-3631
www.richmanpoormancayucos.com

THREE SPECKLED HENS
P.O. Box 850
Templeton, CA 93465
(805) 674-7807
antiques@threespeckledhens.com

TONKADALE GREENHOUSES
3739 Tonkawood Rd.
Minnetonka, MN 55345
(952) 938-6480
www.tonkadale.com

VILLAGE ANTIQUE MART
126 E. Branch St.
Arroyo Grande, CA 93420
(805) 489-6528

VINEYARD ANTIQUE MALL
2320 Ramada
Paso Robles, CA 93446
(805) 237-4012

WEB OF CHARLOTTE
Linda Crain
5215 E. Main St.
Maple Plain, MN 55359
(763) 479-323

Index

Index note: page references in *italics* indicate a photograph.

A

Abacus, as towel holder, *142, 143*
Adirondack chairs:
    country-style porches, *14, 16, 17*
    in family camps, *142, 146*
    family style patios, *28*
    in romantic outdoor sleeping room, *136*
Alphabet letters, oversized, *58, 61, 65, 106*
Aluminum baking pans, *131*
Apple bobbing, *131*
Apple picker candle holder, *149, 150*
Art supplies, storing/displaying, *41*
Ashtrays, repurposing, 44, *44, 73*

B

Baby forks, *131*
Backyards:
    children's fairy tale play area, 68–73
    container gardens in, *80, 81, 82, 83*
    grassless/industrial elegance, 80–83
    gravel and concrete pavers, *66, 80, 81, 81, 82, 83, 83*
    as outdoor rooms, 66–85
    poolside, 74, 75, *75,* 76, *76,* 77, 78, *78, 79*
    reclining/sleeping areas, *69, 72*
    as spa experience, 76, *76, 77*
    sugar'n'spice play area, 68, *68, 69, 70, 71, 71, 72, 73, 73*
    urban industrial elegance, *80,* 81, *81, 82, 83, 83*
    vintage poolside decor, 74, *75, 75*
    See also Cooking outdoors; Dining al fresco
Badges, *102*
Bamboo wind chime, *174, 177*
Barkcloth drapery panel, *112*
Barn wood walls, *58, 61, 65*
Bathing under the stars, 140, 141, *141*
Benches:
    as coffee tables, *12*
    hay bale, *18, 19, 19*
Beverage stations:
    family-style patio, *28, 29, 31*
    farm-style picnic, *130*
    gravel and concrete backyard, *66, 80*
    summertime patios, 44, *44*
Bike tire rims, *9*
Bird feeders, *12, 81*
Birdcages, *140,* 141
Blankets, vintage, *69, 71, 72, 75*
Bolts, embellishing with, *36, 38, 186, 186*
Boot scraper photo holder, *40*
Box-top side table, *136, 137*
Bricks, *52, 53*
Button board tray, *123, 192, 192*

C

Cable spool tables, *32, 36, 38, 186, 186*
Candles:
    apple picker holder, *149, 150*
    bottle bud vase holders, *120*
    bowl and dish holders, *127*
    car jack candle holder, *81*
    dining al fresco, *108*
    drip coffeepot holders, *141*
    electric heater holders, *8, 9*
    enamel coffeepot holder, *63*
    fire extinguisher holders, *30*
    glass pitcher hurricane lamps, *43*
    golf ball caddy hurricane, *132, 133, 138*
    metal bases as holders, *64*
    mismatched glassware holders, *108, 110, 111, 112*
    poolside spa experience, *76, 77*
    ship lantern holders, *77*
    shot glass holders, *55*
    terra cotta pot holders, *177, 179*
    Victorian shelf rest holders, *45*
Car jack candle holders, *81*
Car ramp plant stands, *81, 82*
Cast-iron cooker, *107*
Cattle brands, as house numbers, *11, 180*
Chain link gate, *149, 151, 155*
Chandelier, wire basket, *108, 116,* 117, *117*
Cheese boxes, *63, 90*
Chicken coop potting shed:
    architectural accents, *161*
    potting table/work area, *159, 160,* 161, *161*
    seating area, *159, 162, 164*
    seed and bulb storage, *163*
    shutter shelves, *164,* 165, *165*
    storage ideas, *159,* 161, *163, 163, 164,* 165, *165*
Chicken waterers:
    as candle holders, *77*
    for seed and bulb storage, *163*
Chimineas, *32, 34, 35*
Chisel wind chimes, *148, 153, 195, 195*
Christmas tree light reflectors, *40*
Chuck wagon/cowboy cookouts:
    cupboard storage, *100, 106, 106*
    dressing up condiments, *102, 103*
    table settings and decor, *100,* 101, *102, 103, 104, 105*
    tent ambience, *100, 102, 103*
Coal scoop, storing charcoal, *96*
Coat trees:
    outdoor, *142, 145, 149, 151, 152*
    using reclaimed materials, *34, 35*
    wooden pitch forks, *64, 65*
Cod pole picture frame, *144, 194, 194*
Coffee service, *45, 130*
Coffee table, stacking steel crates, *62*
Container gardens in backyards, *80, 81, 82, 83*

Contemporary outdoor kitchens:
    fully equipped, *86, 87, 88, 89*
    junk-style accessories, *88, 89, 90, 91, 92, 93, 93*
Contemporary style entrance/entryway, 8, *8, 9*
Cooking outdoors:
    contemporary outdoor kitchens, 86–93
    cowboy/chuck wagon, 100–107
    drill bit skewers, *97*
    poolside, 94–99
    storage space, *99, 190, 190*
    tent ambience, *102, 103*
Corkscrews, *22*
Cottage look entrances/entryways, 10, 11, *11, 12,* 13, *13*
Country style:
    colors of, *4*
    entrances/entryways, 14, 15, *15,* 16, *16, 17, 18,* 19, *19*
    porches, *58,* 59, *59,* 60, *60,* 61, *62,* 63, *63,* 64, 65, *65*
Cowboy/chuck wagon cookouts:
    cupboard storage, *100, 106, 106*
    dressing up condiments, *102, 103*
    table settings and decor, *100,* 101, *102, 103, 104, 105*
    tent ambience, *100, 102, 103*
Croquet set, repurposing, *128,* 131
Crystals:
    city sidewalk entryway sparkle, *20,* 22, *24, 25, 25*
    wire basket chandelier, *116,* 117, *117*
Cupboard, chuck wagon, *100, 106, 106*
Cupolas, *130,* 131
Cutlery, vintage, *82*
Cymbals, *9*

D

Dental bowl, repurposing, *170, 171*
Dining al fresco:
    candlelight, *108*
    chairs and seating, *108, 111,* 114, *120, 121, 122, 124, 126*
    farm life picnic, *126, 127, 127, 128, 129, 129, 130, 131, 131*
    framing dining area, *120, 121*
    individual salt and pepper shakers, *125*
    kids' wagon picnic table, *129, 129, 193, 193*
    lakeside inspiration, *110, 110, 111, 112,* 113, *113,* 114, *114, 115*
    rolling up sushi, *125*
    suburban modern, *118,* 119, *119,* 120, *120, 121, 122, 123, 123,* 124, *125, 125*
    wire basket chandelier, *108, 116,* 117, *117*
Domino soap dish, *91, 92, 93, 93*
Door wreath, vintage grate, *24,* 25, *25, 184, 184*
Doorknobs, *112, 113*
Drill bit skewers, *97*
Drum and tire table, *53*

E

Egg carriers, as candleholders, 55
Electric heater parts, 8, 8, 9
Enamel cooker, as storage space, 99
Enamel pot planters, 60, 187, 187
Enamelware, 102, 131
Entrances/entryways:
    city sidewalks, 20, 21, 21, 22, 22, 23, 24, 25, 25
    country style, 4, 14, 15, 15, 16, 16, 17, 18, 19, 19
    modern/contemporary, 6, 6, 7
    seasonal, 4, 5–13
    sitting nook, 12, 13
    spring fling, 6, 6, 7
    summer cottage look, 10, 11, 11, 12, 13, 13
    winter/festive city doors, 20, 21, 21, 22, 22, 23, 24, 25, 25
Eyeglasses, 73

F

Fairy gardens, 70, 188, 188
Family-style patio:
    adult and kid spaces, 28, 29, 32, 33
    outdoor/kidproof items in, 28, 30, 31, 32, 33, 34, 35
    roasting marshmallows, 34, 35
    in two-tiered space, 26, 28
Faucet handles, as bird feeders, 12
Feed sack pillow covers, 135
Fire extinguishers, as candle holders, 30
Fish scaler lamp, 54, 55, 55
Fishing reels, 67
Flashlights, old-fashioned, 136, 144
Flatware:
    baby forks as handles, 131
    fork as Zen garden mini-rake, 178, 178
    holster caddies, 100, 105
    silver salt spoon embellishment, 63
Flower arrangements:
    on country porches, 58, 59
    juice glass tussie-mussie, 113
    in outdoor sleeping area, 136, 137, 151, 152, 153, 154, 155
    ship lantern vases, 77
    in three-tiered serving piece, 44
    Victorian shelf rest vases, 45
Frame and drawer window boxes, 10, 11, 183, 183

G

Galvanized buckets, 31, 107
Galvanized tin vase covers, 56, 57, 57
Garden art:
    HVAC decorative garden stakes, 7, 182, 182
    Welded Waldo, 12
Gardening:
    milk crate cart, 84, 85, 85
    plant markers, 157
    See also Chicken coop potting shed; Meditation garden; Seaside garden
Gas lanterns, 12, 13
Gauges, 30, 31, 171
Gear molds, 22, 23
Glass bottles:
    coat or hat trees with, 34, 35
    collections of, 95
    embellishing, 63
    marshmallow and cracker storage, 33
    urine collection bottle, 151, 152, 155
Glass frogs, 41

Glass pitcher hurricane lamps, 43
Gnomes, 49, 61
Grates, decorating door wreaths, 24, 25, 25, 184, 184
Greenery:
    in meditation garden, 172, 173, 175, 179
    winter/festive doorways, 20, 21, 22, 22, 23, 24, 25, 25
Greenhouses, junk-style:
    chicken coop potting shed, 158–65
    meditation garden, 172–79
    seaside garden, 166–71

H

Hanging scales, 21
Hat trees:
    using reclaimed materials, 34, 35
    wooden pitch forks, 64, 65
Hay bales:
    bench, 18, 19, 19
    sideboard, 128, 130, 131
Holiday trees, entryway, 21, 21, 22, 23
Holly, 20, 22, 22
Holsters, as flatware caddies, 100, 105
Horse muzzle planters, 120, 122
Horseshoes, 107
Hose reels:
    as outdoor dessert cart, 114, 115
    storing logs in, 89
Hot water bottles, recycling, 167
HVAC decorative garden stakes, 7, 182, 182

J

Jewelry:
    embellishing photographs, 72
    napkin rings using, 109
Juice glasses, tussie-mussie, 113
Junking/junk style:
    Junker's toolbox, 181
    little junk gems, 22, 40, 63, 73, 107, 131, 144, 177
    mixing and matching, 17
    rock star junking, 123
    seasonal, 6
Junk-style greenhouses:
    chicken coop potting shed, 158, 158, 159, 160, 161, 161, 162, 163, 164, 165, 165
    meditation garden, 172, 173, 173, 174, 174, 175, 176, 176, 177, 178, 178, 179
    seaside garden, 166, 167, 167, 168, 168, 169, 170, 171, 171

K

Keys, 5, 22
Kool-Aid pitchers, 76, 77

L

Lampshade frames:
    canopy, 69, 72
    glass food containers, 98
    as towel holders, 140, 141
Lights/lighting:
    fish scaler lamp, 54, 55, 55
    wire basket chandelier, 108, 116, 117, 117
    See also Candles
Linens, vintage:
    in child's play area, 69, 71, 72
    cooking outdoors, 97
    outdoor sleeping areas, 132, 134, 138
    pillow coverings, 127
    storage of, 136

Lucite drawer pulls, holding chopsticks, 119
Luggage, linen and towel storage, 136

M

Mail boxes, holiday decorating, 22
Mail pouches, 58, 63
Mason jars, 33
Matchstick holders, 107
Medical supplies, repurposing, 152, 155, 158
Meditation garden:
    hand-crated Zen garden, 178, 178, 179, 197, 197
    incense holders, 177
    tool station, 176, 176, 177
    twine accents, 172, 174, 176, 177
    wall of green, 172, 175
    Zen stones, 177
Metal chairs:
    modern/contemporary entryways, 6, 6, 7
    retro bouncy chairs, 108, 111
    in urban outdoor space, 66, 80
Milk crate gardening carts, 84, 85, 85
Miner's lantern, vintage, 172, 173
Miniature saddles, 104
Minnow bucket planters, 171
Motel chairs, 32, 33

N

Napkin holders, 87
Napkin rings:
    blade of grass and floral pin, 109
    Navy belt, 154, 155
    watch band, 125
Napkins, vintage, 114
Navy belt napkin rings, 154, 155

O

Oil cans, repurposing, 178, 179
Open-air dining:
    farm picnic, 126–31
    lakeside inspiration, 110–117
    suburban modern setting, 118–25
Organ pipe holders, repurposing, 177
Outdoor kitchens:
    chuck wagon cookout, 100–107
    contemporary, 88–93
    poolside cooking, 94–99
Outdoor sleeping retreats:
    bathing under the stars, 140, 141, 141
    family camp, 142–47
    midday snooze area, 148–55
    romantic, 132–41

P

Paint buckets, 22
Painters easel, in patio settings, 41
Patios:
    beverage stations, 44, 44
    creating outdoor spaces, 27
    enclosed, 36–41
    family festivities, 26, 28, 28, 29, 29, 30, 30, 31, 32, 33, 33, 34, 34, 35
    floral arrangements, 36, 37, 39
    rain barrel umbrella stand, 26, 28, 185, 185
    sanctuary for tea, 36–41
    seating, 26, 28, 32, 36, 42, 46
    summertime living, 42–47
    on two-tiered space, 28–35
    weatherproof and kidproof, 28–35
Pedestal sink, backyard beverage station, 80

Photographs:
  boot scraper holder, *40*
  cod pole frame, *144, 194, 194*
  embellishing with jewelry, *72*
  hanging from metal display racks, *51, 52*
Picnic table:
  kids' wagon table, 129, *129*, 193, *193*
  rope bed, *146, 147*
Picture frame ticking headboard, *132, 134, 138, 139, 139*
Pillow coverings:
  feed sack, *135*
  vintage map towels as, *27, 32*
Pinecones, 22, *23*
Pink flamingoes, 94, 95, 98, 99
Pizza cutters, *88*
Place card holders, *105*
Planters:
  bath heater tank, *140, 141*
  enamel pot, *60, 187, 187*
  frame and drawer, *10, 11, 183, 183*
  garden étagère, *149, 151, 152, 153*
  hanging grocer scales, *63*
  horse muzzles, *120, 122*
  metal trash baskets as, *95*
  minnow buckets, *171*
  PVC pipe, *39*
  railroad cart, *83*
  tubs as, *69, 70*
  using dish strainers, *40*
  wooden crate fairy gardens, *70, 188, 188*
Plates:
  as garden decor, *82, 83*
  Madge and Merrill, *144*
  outdoor cooking, *98*
  from restaurant supply, *113*
Playground pieces, *34, 35*
Poker caddy, holding spices, *90*
Porches:
  country style, *14–19, 58–65*
  seating, *4, 12, 14, 15, 48, 51, 58, 59, 61*
  three-season, 50, *50*, 51, 52, *52*, *53–54*, 55, *55*
  welcoming features of, *60, 61, 62, 63, 64–65*
Potting tables, *81, 159, 160, 161, 161*
Printer's drawer tables, *42, 46, 47, 47*

R

Railroad cart planters, *83*
Rain barrel umbrella stand, *26, 28, 185, 185*
Rakes, *15, 18, 19*
Recipe card holders, *90*
Refrigerator enamel drawers, as storage, *144, 146*
Restaurant supplies:
  plates and dishes, *113, 114*
  repurposing, 52, *54*
Riding boots, festive entryways, *20, 21*
Road markers, *81*

S

Saddles, miniature, *104*
Salt and pepper shakers:
  individual, *125*
  souvenir, *144, 194, 194*
Sand and rock Zen garden, 178, *178, 179*, 197, *197*
Scaffolding buffet, *99, 190, 190*
Schoolhouse paper cutter, as pizza cutter, *88*
Scooter beverage/ice bucket, 28, *29, 31*
Seaside garden:
  dental bowl watering station, *170, 171*

driftwood table, *166*
hanging buoy accents, *169*
helping hands, *166, 167, 196, 196*
as playful Helga's house, 167, *167*, 168, *168, 169*
scaffolding defining space, *169*
shell-concoction octopus, *168, 169*
toolbox herb garden, *170*
Shot glass candle holders, *55*
Shot puts, *177, 179*
Showerhead wind chime, *174, 177*
Signs, vintage, 34, 39, 40, *101*
Silver salt spoons, *63*
Skateboard/stirrup towel holder, *106, 107, 191, 191*
Sleeping bags, retro, *144*
Sleeping under the stars:
  beverage/refreshment center, *149, 151, 152, 155*
  chisel wind chimes, *148, 153, 195, 195*
  family camp, *142, 143, 143, 144, 144, 145, 146, 146, 147*
  midday snooze, 148, *148, 149, 150, 150, 151, 152, 152, 153, 154, 154, 155*
  picnic table rope bed, *146, 147*
  retro sleeping bags, *144*
  romantic retreat, *132, 133, 134, 135, 135, 136, 137, 137, 138, 139, 139, 140, 141, 141*
  rubber tire privacy wall, *149, 152, 154*
  swinging bed, *132, 134*, 135
  ticking headboard, *138, 139, 139*
  twilight bathing, *140, 141, 141*
Soap dish, domino, *91, 92, 93, 93*
Spice holder, *90*
Spinning game wheel, as lazy Susan, *102, 103*
Spool tables, *32, 36, 38, 186, 186*
Sprinkler heads, *45*
Stirrup/skateboard towel holder, *106, 107, 191, 191*
Storage:
  camping, *144, 146*
  linen and towels, *136*
  outdoor cooking, *99, 190, 190*
  potting shed, *159, 161, 163, 164, 165, 165*
  wine, *50, 104*
Swimming pools:
  backyard styles, 74, 75, *75*, 76, *76, 77*, 78, *78, 79*
  cart towel holders, *78*
  poolside cooking, 94, 95, *95, 96, 97, 97, 98, 98, 99*
  as spa experience, 76, *76, 77, 79*
  tripod torches, *79, 189, 189*
  vintage decor, 74, 75, *75*

T

Tables:
  box-top side table, *136, 137*
  cable spool, *32, 36, 38, 186, 186*
  enameled heater, *95*
  inverted stool with glass top, *162, 163*
  kids' wagon picnic table, 129, *129*, 193, *193*
  stacking steel crates, *62*
  stump side tables, *124, 125*
  tire and drum, *53*
  using printer's drawers and washboards, *42, 46, 47, 47*
  wheel well side tables, *32*
Tabletop runner, using barkcloth drapery, *112*
Tea for two patio:
  cozy furniture, *36, 38*

displaying art supplies, *41*
enclosed sanctuary for, *36, 37, 38*
junk gems, *40*
junk-style tea service, *39*
Telephone stands, *44*
Thermometers, *10*
Thread holders, 22, *22*
Three-tiered serving pieces, repurposing, 44, *44*
Ticking headboard, *138, 139, 139*
Tins, vintage, *88*
Tires:
  drum and tire table, *53*
  rubber tire privacy wall, *149, 152, 154*
Towel holders:
  globe stand as, *55*
  kindergarten abacus, *142, 143*
  lampshade frame as, *140, 141*
  poolside carts for, *78*
  skateboard/stirrup, *106, 107, 191, 191*
Train cases, *145*
Tripod torches, *79, 189, 189*
Trunks, 42, *43, 58, 65*
Tub planters, *69, 70*
Twine, embellishing with, *36, 38, 186, 186*

U

Umbrella stand, rain barrel, *26, 28, 185, 185*
Urinals, repurposing, *152, 155*

V

Vases:
  galvanized tin covers, *56, 57, 57*
  See also Flower arrangements
Vents, *9*
Vintage clothespin bag, as wine bucket, *123*
Vintage fabrics, *18, 19, 19*
Vintage glasses, *29*
Vintage map towels:
  as pillow coverings, *27, 32*
Vintage scales, *21*

W

Wagon picnic table, 129, *129*, 193, *193*
Washboards, 8, *8, 42, 46, 47, 47*
Washers, embellishing with, *36, 38, 186, 186*
Watches/watch faces, 22, *69, 70, 73, 125*
Watering cans, *11, 176*
Welded Waldo, *12*
Wheel wells, as side tables, *32*
Wind chimes:
  chisel, *148, 153, 195, 195*
  showerhead, *174, 177*
Windmills, *16, 17*
Window boxes, frame and drawer, *10, 11, 183, 183*
Windows, patio sophistication, *39*
Wine cask table tops, 28, *29, 185, 185*
Wine holders, *50, 104, 131, 145*
Wire basket chandelier, 108, *116, 117, 117*
Wooden crate:
  as coffee tote, *130*
  planting fairy gardens in, *70, 188, 188*
Wreath, vintage grate, 24, *25, 25, 184, 184*

Z

Zen garden, handcrafted sand and rock, 178, *178, 179, 197, 197*